Affirming the Soul:

Remarkable Conversations Between
Mental Health Professionals
and
an Ordained Minister

Affirming the Soul:

Remarkable Conversations Between Mental Health Professionals and an Ordained Minister

by Rev. Jeffrey H. Boyd, M.D.

With Preface and Comments by Krister Stendahl

and "Illusion of a Future" by Oskar Pfister

Soul Research Institute
Cheshire, Connecticut

Scripture quotations marked (NRSV) are taken from the *New Revised Standard Version Bible,* copyright © 1989 by the Division of Christian Education of the National Council of the Churches of Christ in the United States of America. Used by permission.

Cover design: Lana Kleinschmidt
Editor: Fenwick Anderson

Published by the Soul Research Institute
P.O. Box 89, Cheshire, CT 06410

10 9 8 7 6 5 4 3 2 1

Manufactured in the United States of America

Publisher's Cataloging in Publication

(Prepared by Quality Books Inc.)

Boyd, Jeffrey H.
    Affirming the soul : remarkable conversations between mental health professionals and an ordained minister / by Jeffrey H. Boyd
; with preface and comments by Krister Stendahl.
    Includes: Illusion of a future / by Oskar Pfister.
    Includes bibliographical references.
    Preassigned LCCN: 93-93584.
    ISBN 0-9636990-3-2
    1. Soul. 2. Psychiatry and religion. 3. Mental health personnel—Interviews. I. Title.

BT741.2.B69 1994   128'.1
                                    QBI93-21919

Table of Contents

Comparing the King James Version of 1611 to the New Revised Standard Version of 1989:

For I have satiated the weary **soul**, and I have replenished every sorrowful **soul**.

(KJV: Jeremiah 31:25)

I will satisfy the weary, and all who are faint I will replenish.

(NRSV: Jeremiah 31:25)

Preface

by Krister Stendahl

Jeffrey Boyd was a student of mine at Harvard Divinity School a quarter of a century ago. By then, theologians had decided that "soul" was a misleading word that should be avoided. After his theological training, he was ordained in the Episcopal Church. He has told me how during prayers he thought he heard God calling him to write a book on the soul. He could not imagine undertaking this "Mission: Impossible" because he thought that psychiatrists were treating the soul. To prepare himself to write this book, Boyd got trained in the mental health field. First he was trained at the Carl Jung Institute in Zürich. Then he spent four years in medical school at Case Western Reserve, where he received an M.D. For the next four years he was trained in psychiatry at Yale Medical School. Seven years he was on the faculty of the National Institute of Mental Health. After that he was on the Yale psychiatry faculty. Now he is chair of psychiatry at a large hospital in Connecticut. When he was in psychoanalysis himself, he rediscovered who he was, namely the author of a book not yet written: *Affirming the Soul*.

He still leads worship services and is involved as an Episcopal minister. After a quarter-century, Dr. Boyd finally felt prepared to write the book to which he felt called twenty-five years earlier. *Affirming the Soul*, consisting of interviews with mental health experts, shows rich insights into how the soul might be understood in our time.

Of the many pearls in this book, one of the most fascinating is meeting Oskar Pfister, a Lutheran pastor in Zürich. When Freud wrote "Future of an Illusion," he apologized to his close friend Pfister. Freud was delighted when Pfister offered to write a rebuttal, which Freud arranged to have printed in his main journal *Imago*. Pfister's article went by the somewhat humorous title "Illusion of a Future." He wanted to ridicule the Enlightenment notion that science was making this fallen world unambiguously better and better. Pfister's article had a profound impact on Freud, and has shaped the mental health attitude toward religion ever since. In the duel between "Future of an Illusion" and "Illusion of a Future," it could even be said that the latter article won the battle. Yet it has never before been translated into English. Dr. Boyd has translated it as part of this book.

I have been encouraging him over a period of years, since I have found my conversations with him stimulating. And it is obvious to me that there are values and overtones and undertones in the word soul that could be reclaimed on the threshold of the Twenty-First Century. That is the more possible since more and more people are far removed from "platonic" distinctions between body and soul. And in these matters — as in so many others — African-American spirituals and spirituality have given new intensity to the word soul.

Perhaps it should be stressed that the issue is not "what is the correct translation" of the biblical words that English translators for centuries rendered by "soul": the Hebrew *nefesh* and the Greek *psyche*. As cultures change and the habits of thinking and speaking change, the translator must find new approximations to what the original might have meant in the ears of its hearers. For example, the *King James Version's* "conversation" in Philippians 3:20 is Seventeenth Century language and refers to where one moves about but to us it suggests talking. Hence, we now correctly read in the *Revised Standard Version*: our commonwealth is in heaven (Greek: *politeuma*). In a similar way, avoiding "soul" in more recent translations was necessary when "soul" suggested the precious opposite to the despicable body. But something was lost by such an educational move, and that is what Jeff Boyd wants to recapture and reclaim.

For such an enterprise of restoration I would take my point of departure in Genesis 2:7: "Then the LORD God formed the Human (*ha-adam*) of dust from the ground (*min-ha-adama*) and breathed into its nostrils the breath of life, and the Human (*ha-adam*) became a living soul (*nefesh*)." Thus the human reality is not the split of body and soul but the new wholeness of the <u>soul</u>: Matter + God's Spirit = The Living Soul. Such a model of wholeness should not be lost. It gives dignity and it hallows matter — as an artist creates beauty out of clay. It reminds us of our frailty, for we carry God's treasure in earthen vessels as Paul liked to put it (2 Corinthians 4:7).

The Jewish translators of the Hebrew Bible into Greek felt that the best word for *nefesh* was *psyche*, which meant both life and soul. The biblical context made it clear that <u>soul</u> meant the living being. When ministers and priests say that their congregation or parish has so and so many souls, they are not referring to the "soul part" of their parishioners. They mean people. They speak in biblical, not in religious terms.

Jeff Boyd's dogged enthusiasm in redeeming the soul-language deserves serious attention and the interviews he reports are powerful evidence of the need for better models of wholeness toward healing. I do believe <u>soul</u> is a word ready to be reclaimed in order to revive our understanding of ourselves and our relation to God — what Jeff Boyd refers to as an analogy to the Copernican revolution of human consciousness.

Krister Stendahl
September 1993

Comparing the King James Version of 1611 to the New Revised Standard Version Bible of 1989:

Let every **soul** be subject unto the higher powers.   *(KJV: Romans 13:1)*

Let every **person** be subject to the governing authorities.   *(NRSV: Romans 13:1)*

Chapter 1
Soul Murder

"Soul is a word I use a lot," Alan said. Like me, Rev. Alan Broadhead, M.D., is a psychiatrist and an ordained minister in the Episcopal Church.

"Although I am not exactly sure how to define the soul," he said, "I guess I would think it is us in our entirety, our identity. It is also the transcendent side of us, the part that belongs to the commonwealth in Heaven. For example, I now run an adolescent ward of a state mental hospital here in North Dakota. The staff is preoccupied with the physical and sexual abuse that occurred in our patients' lives. I don't mean to underestimate that. But that kind of abuse is slight by comparison with the soul murder which has occurred in the lives of these patients."

"Soul murder?" I asked.

"It means the utter destruction of a human personality," he said. "Some of these kids I treat in the hospital have been so crucified, so badly beaten by life, that no one but Christ has gone through what they have gone through. My staff wants to know whether there was incest, and how often, and whether there was penetration. I think the important thing was not the physical nor the sexual abuse, but the brutalization.

"We had a patient just the other day that was so obnoxious that the staff hated him. But I didn't hate him. I listened quietly to his abuse. People couldn't understand why

I tolerated such vitriolic language. I said that I imagine that when I die and get up to the gates of Heaven, I will find this patient standing there along with St. Peter, making a decision about whether I get in or not. This child is the crucified one. He is closer to Christ, in terms of the savage murder that he has endured, than I will ever be. My evaluation by God will be determined by how I treat this unpleasant teenager."

"So he is a representative of Christ," I asked, "on earth today? That reminds me how you always give money to beggars, even though you know most of them are alcoholics or drug addicts."

"I still do," he said.

"How do you treat soul murder?" I asked.

"Resurrection is what is required," he replied. "Treating a damaged soul is not enough. Because these teenagers in the state hospital haven't just been damaged. They have been murdered."

"Resurrection?" I am always astonished with the way this man thinks. "How?"

"We have to recognize the soul," he said. "Otherwise we will perpetuate the soul murder which has been the theme in these kids' lives. I don't mean it in any narrow religious sense. We have to see that we are dealing with something that transcends emotional abuse. These kids aren't just physical and emotional. We have to see the transcendent side of them."

"I still don't see how you treat soul murder," I said.

"Half the adolescents I treat are Native American — Sioux — and half are Anglo," he said. "The Native Americans right now are going through a revival of their religion. That's why I've been reading Black Elk's books. In addition to *Black Elk Speaks*, one of the elders of the tribe has given me an earlier book, *The Sacred Pipe* by Black Elk. It describes the different ceremonies of the sacred pipe and the sun dance. I strongly encourage the Native American youngsters in my inpatient unit to learn more about the Sioux religion, to get involved in it."

"Why?" I asked.

"For the same reason that I encourage the Anglo teenagers to seek something more than just drugs and alcohol. Because there is something more to life. It is what I preach in the parish."

"Surely you don't preach the Sioux religion to your Native American patients?" I asked.

"No," he said. "Let me give you an example of what I am talking about. The staff tends to get into power struggles with these kids. They punish patients who break the rules. These teenagers have always been breaking the rules. They have lived brutal lives. They are defiant, oppositional. The staff's attitude just perpetuates the same punitive pattern. Before I came to work here the inpatient unit used ninety hours per month of locking patients in seclusion rooms or tying them down in four-point restraints on the bed. Today we use zero hours per month. That is because I approach things differently."

"How?" I asked.

"Yesterday," he said, "there was a kid who habitually violated every rule. The teenager threw a plate of food across the dining room. It smashed against the wall. There was food all over the floor. By the time I arrived the staff was standing on one side of this mess on the floor. On the other side was the patient. It was a tense confrontation. The staff was insisting that the patient clean it up. Predictably, the patient refused. When I looked at the patient, I could see that it was impossible for her to clean it up. Nor was it possible for the staff to clean it up. So I cleaned it up. I got the paper towels and I began to clean up the food on the floor. Instantly, the patient and the staff helped me."

"Did that help the patient's soul murder?" I asked.

"The patient calmed down. It brought out her humanity," Alan replied. "I simply wanted to show her what God's grace means. It was simply that I was acting on the basis of Paul's idea of justification by faith alone."

"Justification by faith?" I asked. "What does that have to do with a smashed plate of food on the floor?"

"We don't have to do anything," he said, "to deserve God's love. It is simply given to us. That is what I was trying to demonstrate by my behavior in cleaning up the food on the floor."

"Justification by faith?" I asked again.

"Before I went through my own psychoanalysis I couldn't appreciate what Paul was talking about when he said, 'Justification by faith and not by works,'" Alan said. "I had an oppressive superego. It was necessary for me to do concrete things in order to feel worthy as a human being. But after I went through psychoanalysis I no longer needed to prove myself worthy. I was able to feel self-esteem without accomplishing anything. I could accept that God has already done all the work, and was reaching out to me. In the parable of the Prodigal Son, it was the father who rushed down the stairs and ran out to meet his wayward son in order to be generous to him. That is how God is. In the standoff between the staff and the patient over the smashed plate of food on the floor, all I was trying to demonstrate was what God's grace means on a practical level. I was acting in the generous and forgiving way that God acts toward me."

"I am reminded about what you told me before," I said, "about running an inpatient psychiatry ward on the model of the Suffering Servant."

"Yes," he replied. "It's the same thing."

After Dr. Broadhead had trained in psychiatry in England, he migrated to the United States, where he was trained in a second psychiatry residency at the Institute of Living in Hartford. In that hospital, he once ran an inpatient unit for disturbed adolescent girls. The patients kept precipitating battles for control with the nursing staff. They would act out and break the rules, and the nursing staff would respond by "setting limits," i.e. by engaging in a battle for control. Alan had decided to introduce some ideas he found in the Book of Isaiah, particularly the idea of the servant (Isaiah 41:9, 42:1-9, 49:1-7, 50:4-11, 52:13-53:12). "It is the servant who really is in control," Alan told me. Without talking in religious jargon, he gently introduced the idea that the staff should see themselves in the role of servants to these disturbed adolescents. At first the nursing staff rebelled against this notion. They thought it preposterous. But slowly a new culture took root. What resulted was a transformation of the atmosphere on the unit. The whole place calmed down. A sense of tranquility and peace settled in, which was unknown earlier. Furthermore, the patients then began to focus on their psychological problems, once the distraction of an uproar on the ward was removed.

"It means getting away from the primitive superego type of religion," Alan said. "The staff in my hospital take the stance that they will punish the patient who breaks the rules. They want to give patients more privileges only when the patient earns it based on improved behavior. But my attitude is to give the reward first, before it is deserved."

"What do you mean?" I asked.

"The other day we had a patient who is always defiant, rebellious," Alan said. "The staff kept the patient restricted to the inpatient unit, saying her behavior had to improve before she would get more privileges. But I said, 'You know very well her behavior will never improve. If you punish her she will experience herself as continuing to be brutalized here, just like she was in her childhood. I vote we give her the privileges first and see if she doesn't come to deserve them afterwards.' So I let the patient go for walks outside the hospital. And within a week she was acting better than anyone could believe possible. She became more responsible and began to act like someone who deserved to be able to take walks outside the hospital. 'You trust me in a way that no one ever trusted me before,' she said to me. I think what keeps the staff of the hospital from assassinating me is that they can see the patients get better."

I remembered something that Alan had once told me:

"Christ is present to me through the downtrodden, the underdog, and the 'least of these.' When someone is treated unfairly, or human suffering is neglected, I personally suffer. My early childhood sensitized me to the affliction of people who are forgotten."

Like me, Alan thinks of himself as a marginal person, a maverick. He has a visceral level of identification with the outcast. This he regards as a strength he gained from his childhood and from his religion. While his soul was not murdered in his own childhood, it almost was, as described in Chapter 16.

I offered Alan the possibility of using a pseudonym in this chapter. He said he thought he was identifiable whether his name was used or not. Therefore, we agreed I would use his real name.

What Ever Happened
to the Word "Soul"?

"I became interested in finding a word," Alan said, "to capture what I was witnessing in my clinical practice. Child abuse involves a level of destruction beyond any language I could find. The word 'murder' suggested itself, but what I found in my clinical work was worse than 'murder.' Murder of a person's body is something I can tolerate, but what I was witnessing was worse than murder of a body — it was murder of a child's soul. One day it dawned on me that 'soul murder' captures the passion of what has happened to these children. Neither the psychiatric diagnoses of *DSM-3R* [*Editor's note: This is the name of the diagnostic manual used in psychiatry*] nor any of the Freudian language conveys the magnitude of the destruction caused by child abuse. Reaching way back in my memory I remember once having heard the phrase 'soul murder' in one of Ibsen's plays.[1] I began to dip into it. I went to the library and asked the librarian to help me with a literature search. She found quite a few books on soul murder, including a recent one by Leonard Shengold which describes child abuse in that language."[2]

"Can you give me another example?" I asked.

"There is a boy in our psychiatric hospital who suffers from Borderline Personality Disorder," Alan said. "I found in his history that when he was 20 months old there was already evidence of sexual abuse. His anal area had abrasions and bruises. There were bruises all over his body and an unexplained broken arm. By the age of 20 months he was dehydrated and malnourished to the point that his hair was falling out. His early years had been shattered. At the age of four he watched her father beat his sister to death. His baby sister had been crying. The father responded by bludgeoning the infant to death.

"That kind of a childhood bespeaks the destruction of anything that is good. It is such an overwhelming story that the word 'murder' isn't enough to capture the enormity of it. One needs a word beyond 'spirit' to describe what was destroyed in this boy. The psychiatric jargon words like 'self' or 'ego' seem so sanitized, and don't really capture at a visceral level what was destroyed in this patient. I have a sense that psychiatrists and psychologists are groping toward some word to convey what their clinical work is about, at precisely the moment when the word 'soul' has been discredited by the theologians."

I had been talking with Alan about why theologians no longer use the word "soul." Indeed, the word is often considered a toxic waste dump of dualism that must be avoided if we are true to biblical religion. "Soul" was considered too much a dualistic word, suggesting a division between soul and body. The word "soul" was a casualty of the battle between two schools of theologians: the so-called "Resurrectionists" versus the so-called "Immortalists."[3] Leaders of the Resurrectionist school, Oscar Cullmann and Krister Stendahl, said there was no immortal soul found in the New Testament. The Resurrectionists, who won the theological war, thought the Immortalists owned the word "soul."

"I can't believe these theologians have discarded the word 'soul,'" Alan said. "There is no other word that can replace 'soul.' Certainly we have no psychological word capable of replacing the word 'soul.'

"This boy is now a teenager," Alan said. "He has the affective lability and moodiness and suicidality which is typical of Borderlines. He is a broken person. He is prematurely sexually mature, while at the same time he is incapable of living in society. When a young woman is sexually interested, he knows exactly what to do. But he knows nothing of *agape*. He is needy and has become my shadow, studying every detail of my life. Of course he does that in a teasing, taunting, abusive and angry way. But I think that fundamentally he is searching for a complete human being.

"If you go back to Margaret Mahler's work on separation and individuation,"[4] he continued, "you find that is precisely the stage of development at which this boy's life has been destroyed. Patients with Borderline Personality Disorder have been soul-murdered.[5] By this term I mean the complete destruction of the human personality. The term 'sexual abuse' or 'child abuse' or 'destruction of the self' or 'absence of ego' doesn't capture the enormity of it."

Comparing the King James Version of 1611 to the New Revised Standard Version of 1989:

Thou fool, this night thy **soul** shall be required of thee.   *(KJV: Luke 12:20)*

You fool! This very night your **life** is being demanded of you.   *(NRSV: Luke 12:20)*

Comparing the KJV to the NRSV:

But whoso committeth adultery with a woman lacketh understanding: he that doeth it destroyeth his own **soul.**

(KJV: Proverbs 6:32)

But he who commits adultery has no sense; he who does it destroys himself.

(NRSV: Proverbs 6:32)

Chapter 2
Comment by Krister Stendahl

"I like the way your book begins by discussing soul murder," said Professor Krister Stendahl. He was my New Testament teacher. Stendahl is former dean of the Harvard Divinity School, and retired bishop of Stockholm's Swedish Lutheran Church. We spoke at his home on October 20, 1992, and again on Nantucket, July 29, 1993.

"That is high-voltage stuff," Stendahl continued. "You are not just talking about parlor-game psychology. You are talking about serious psychiatric illness, about what the New Testament would consider to be demons and evil. Have you thought about demons at all?"

"No way am I going to speak about demons," I replied. "It is difficult enough to try to write a book about the soul when nobody but nobody wants to use that word. Theologians avoid it as a misleading word. Mental health experts hate the word because it sounds like religion is trying to stake out a claim in what they regard as their territory. Forget the stuff about demons, Krister. My book is controversial enough just talking about the soul."

"Maybe you don't have to say it," he replied. "Just leave it to the reader's imagination. The point is that you are not just talking about nice ideas, you are talking about high-voltage religion in this first chapter. It is a chapter about an adolescent man with Borderline Personality Disorder whose life was shattered. He suffered soul murder. But I see a problem with your book.

"In subsequent chapters you say that to find one's soul one must lose it, i.e. self-denial," Stendahl continued. "I think you have to distinguish different audiences to whom you speak. If you are speaking to an audience of psychiatric patients with shattered souls, you would not want to preach loss of soul. This man with Borderline Personality Disorder already lost it. His soul was murdered. Such a person needs to be encouraged to feel some self-esteem, to love himself a little, and learn to embrace his soul.

"People sometimes ask me why the Bible talks so much about self-denial," Stendahl said. "My answer is because the people who wrote were usually the people in power. They were speaking to themselves, reminding themselves to be humble. Most of the valuable things in life can't be had by directly going after them. Love, genuine humility, true openness to life, cannot be had by a direct approach. They come as by-products, it seems.

"In any case," he continued, "people whose lives are shattered don't need to be preached self-denial. I like the confessional prayer which is used these days by women, 'I confess that I have not stood up . . . that I have not spoken up . . . .' It is a 'negative' confession."

"So you are suggesting that the Christian message about the soul should be different for different audiences," I asked, "self-affirmation for the downcast, self-denial for the powerful?"

"Exactly," he said, "but too often the 'have-nots' hear only the talk about humility and the 'haves' only the self-affirmation. That is why preaching is so difficult and individual soul care so necessary."

Justification by Faith

"This man Dr. Alan Broadhead sounds like a remarkable man," Stendahl said. "But I want to make a comment about Dr. Broadhead's interpretation of 'justification by faith.' In my old book on Paul I pointed out that Paul didn't have an introspective conscience.[6] When he spoke of 'justification by faith' he was defending the right of the Gentiles to be full and equal Christians, on the same footing as the Jewish Christians of the time. Paul was not talking about relief of a heavy conscience. It was Augustine who initiated the psychological interpretation of Paul's phrase. This psychological interpretation really blossomed in Martin Luther, who was concerned with how to find a gracious God. Thus the idea of having one's plagued conscience relieved was read as analogous to what Paul meant, but it is only an analogy. It is not what Paul thought he was talking about. Thus the phrase 'justification by faith' means two different things, which are analogous to one another.

"In a deep depression," Stendahl said, "justification by faith is a teaching that makes sense. There is evidence that Luther was a depressive. I am sure Paul was not depressed; at least that's not how I read Paul. But again you have to be careful about what audience you are addressing. While 'justification by faith' might be helpful to some people with psychiatric problems, as a general principle it leads to the idea of cheap grace. We see in Martin Luther's preaching on Matthew 5:20 that he was able to distinguish different audiences, and adapt his message accordingly."

Matthew 5:20 says:

For I tell you, unless your righteousness exceeds that of the scribes and Pharisees, you will never enter the kingdom of heaven. (NRSV)

"Luther refers the 'righteousness of the Pharisees' in Matthew 5:20 to the actual moral shortcomings of the citizens of his own city of Wittenberg," Stendahl said. "Can you imagine Luther not taking the opportunity to speak about his favorite theme, justification by faith? Luther applied this verse to the sins and injustices he saw around him right there in Wittenberg. Luther wasn't preaching cheap grace! He didn't think the citizens of Wittenberg could be justified by faith alone. He tailored his message to fit his audience.

"My point is that you need to have great sensitivity about which audience you are addressing when you talk about either:

- Self-denial or
- Justification by faith.

"People who are downcast have already lost their soul. The adolescent man you describe in Chapter 1 has lost his soul. His life is shattered. He is at a nadir. To him you would not speak of self-denial. Rather you would speak of justification by faith.

"The opposite situation is when one is addressing those who are prosperous and doing well, like the citizens of Wittenberg," Stendahl concluded. "To them you would not speak of justification by faith, for you would not want to encourage the idea of cheap grace. That audience should be told that 'whoever wants to save his soul will lose it, but whoever loses his soul for Christ will find it.'"

The Missing Word: "Soul"

"What I think you should do in these boxes," Stendahl said, "where you quote biblical passages about the soul, is to compare the *King James Version* to the *New Revised Standard Version Bible*. The point of the boxes should be to show the reader that this word 'soul' was a prominent part of the Bible throughout history until suddenly in the Twentieth Century when the word disappeared from the Bible almost entirely. Your task, Jeff, is to demonstrate that."

"These boxes remind me," I said, "of a Bible translator who once said to me, 'We think it is better, wherever possible, to use a word other than "soul" to translate the Hebrew word *nephesh* or the Greek word *psyche* into English.' But there are many verses where the *nephesh* or *psyche* have not been translated into any English word in modern Bibles."

"I also think you should change the title of your book," Stendahl said. "I think *Affirming the Soul* is OK as a title," he continued. "But I would prefer it if your title was *Reclaiming the Soul,* or perhaps even better would be *The Soul Reclaimed.* The point is that this word almost dropped out of the Bible in modern translations, but in your book you are bringing it back."

Comparing . . .

Preserve my **soul**.

(KJV: Psalm 86:2)

Preserve my **life**.

(NRSV: Psalm 86:2)

Behold, all **souls** are mine; as the **soul** of the father, so also the **soul** of the son is mine: the **soul** that sinneth, it shall die.

(KJV: Ezekiel 18:4)

Know that all **lives** are mine; the **life** of the parent as well as the **life** of the child is mine: it is only the **person** who sins that shall die.

(NRSV: Ezekiel 18:4)

What Is the Soul?

And so it is written, The first man Adam was made a living **soul**.

(KJV: 1 Corinthians 15:45)

Thus it is written, "The first man, Adam, became a living **being**.

(NRSV: 1 Corinthians 15:45)

Chapter 3
Rachel

Rachel is a psychiatric social worker. She requested that her real name not be used.

1. Psychotherapists Treat the Soul

"I am writing a book on the 'soul' or, in Hebrew, *nephesh*," I said. "I am interviewing a variety of mental health professionals concerning whether the soul, or some aspect of the soul, is what we treat in mental health."

"There are several other people you should interview rather than me," she said. "I am not an expert in this."

"But I want to know what you think," I said. "I am interested in your clinical experience."

"How would you define the *nephesh*?" she asked.

"I'll answer that in a minute, but first let me ask how you would define it," I dodged. "Being a good psychiatrist."

"So, doctor, tell me more about that," she laughed. "No. I'm asking the question. How would you define the *nephesh*?"

"I would stick to the Scriptures," I said. "The word *nephesh* had a wide variety of meanings. But often it was a person's true identity. It was often the whole person, or the whole personality, or the vitality of a breathing organism. It included all the person's emotions, aspirations, and relationships. The word was often used as a personal pronoun, like 'I,' or 'myself.' It is often translated 'person.'"

"My comments come out of a context of Judaism," she said. "'Soul' is one possible translation of *nephesh*, but *nephesh* means more than that. It also means 'life.' *Nephesh* embodies all; it is the essence of what makes us human, what separates us from the animals. It is what God blows into us to make us alive. The whole human being, everything that makes an individual, is denoted. Clinically, I work with Jews. I also work with Jews who want to return to their Judaism after an absence. So you ask whether we treat the *nephesh* in psychotherapy? My answer is Yes, we do treat the *nephesh*. If anything, we don't focus enough attention on treating the *nephesh*. Sometimes we focus too much on the behavioral manifestations and ignore what lies below. In the deeper levels of psychotherapy we reach the level of the *nephesh*. We reach down and affect how clients see themselves.

"Psychotherapists often shy away from spirituality," she continued. "Probably we shouldn't shy away from spirituality. Often our clients are looking for that sort of healing. People are looking for communion with their essence, their essence being the *nephesh*. They want to get in touch with who they really are at their core. Sometimes people turn to outward religion to try to find their essence. But outward religion doesn't always do that for people. Anyway, I want to tell you about several other people who would be more interesting for you to interview than me."

She had stirred up an interesting array of feelings inside me. I felt that her reluctance to talk reflected a certain respect for scholars and a recognition that she was not one. On the other hand, I experienced her as warm, empathic, delightful. And her comments about the *nephesh* struck me as profound.

2. God's View of Our *Nephesh*

Next week I asked her if God's view of her could be known.

"Why do you ask?" she said. "I don't see what that has to do with psychotherapy."

"Maybe it doesn't," I replied. "I sometimes think of my soul as the person God sees me to be. I figure God may know me even better than my psychoanalyst."

She laughed. "Yes," she said.

"So the question naturally arises," I continued, "how am I to know what God's view is."

"I see where you are coming from," she replied. "My gut reaction is yes, God has a view of who I am. Now about gaining access, I think there is access. But I see it as a process as opposed to a finished product, an evolving process. There is often a discrepancy between how I view myself and how God views me. God has a much more positive sense of me. God is more forgiving and has less of a punitive superego than I have. God sees that my capacity is greater than what I have done so far."

"Yes, yes," I said.

"I would even say that the discrepancy between my view and God's view is a measure of mental illness," she said. "For everyone there is some discrepancy, but when the width of the gap is huge, that indicates the pain of mental illness. I know that out there is a vision of me as terrific. When I look at myself, if I don't see that kind of potential, then I'm neurotic. If I feel no potential for my life, that is deeply pathologic. We are always in a process of becoming, evolving in our own growth. God is a personal God. He knows what is going on, and is not disapproving.

"Judaism connects me to something greater than myself," she continued. "It is a very safe feeling, like having a parent out there who loves you. But God is freer than my parents, less neurotic. 'OK,' says God, 'Go ahead, here is what you can become.' Now that could be spiritual in some ways. But in some ways it is not spiritual. It can also be very achievement-oriented in the world.

"When I do psychotherapy with religious clients, or clients with a religious connection, I tell them 'God doesn't make junk.' Clients often feel they are junk. People have a sense that God may come down on them. I try to free up their idea of God, to allow them to see God as less rigid and more forgiving. Now, what was the other part of your question?"

"Can you gain access to how God sees you?" I reminded her.

"You mean me in particular," she queried, "not just how God sees people in general?"

"How God sees Rachel," I clarified.

"Yes," she replied. "I guess the traditional answer would be through prayer. But more than that, through communion with and conversing with God, through my thoughts. I am deeply religious and deeply connected to a Being that is divine. By living my Judaism, that is how I gain this connection, surrounding myself with the symbols, rituals, and people who reinforce that. Mine is not a religion that requires nothing of me. Connecting with the Jewish God requires a life lived in a Jewish way. And when I do that, I have a sense of being coherent, of being centered. It makes me feel very stable in my central core. Here you see the natural connection with psychotherapy."

"What?" I puzzled.

"Because psychotherapy has to do with who we are," she said, "finding out who we are. Freud was overtly hostile to religion, yet he came out of a Jewish background, and his ways of thinking were profoundly Jewish."

"How?" I asked.

"Freud's sense of reflection about who we are," she said. "This is an important part of the Jewish tradition. Like at the High Holy Days we look at what we've done and who we are. We don't reflect on this so that God can come down on us. We review the year in order to become clear about who we are and what we've done. So God can forgive us. There are three important elements: *t'phila* or prayer, *tzedakah* or charity — and by the way, the Hebrew word for charity means justice — and *maasim tovim* or good deeds. So it is not just enough to be repentant. We must also act on the basis of that repentance and do good deeds. What we say is *chesed*, which is a deed that extends you beyond yourself."

"I see," I said. I felt deeply appreciative of her generosity in sharing all this with me.

"So gaining access is partly gained through Jewish education," she continued, "but to get close to God one must enact that which is Judaism, one must participate."

3. A Paradox of the Soul

"I think that to seek your *nephesh* (or 'soul') is to lose it," I said, "whereas to lose your *nephesh* for God's sake is to find it. Jesus said something like this.* Is that a saying that makes any sense to you? Or is it an opaque saying?"

---

* The Gospels say:

> For those who want to save their *psyche* will lose it, and those who lose their *psyche* for my sake will find it (NRSV: Matthew 16:25, Mark 8:35, Luke 9:24, Luke 17:33, John 12:25).

Jesus also advocated losing one's *psyche* in Matthew 10:39 and 20:28; Mark 10:45; Luke 14:26; John 10:11,15,17; and 15:13. In these verses *psyche* is usually translated into English as "life," because of the eschatological expectation of Apocalypse. [*Editor's note: "Eschatological" means the expectation that the world will end soon.*] Martyrdom is the implied focus. But the word *psyche* could also be translated "self" or "soul." This topic is discussed by Professor Krister Stendahl in Chapter 5.

The Aramaic word *nephesh* (נ פ ש) is pronounced the same and has the same meaning as the Hebrew word. We only know from the Greek New Testament what Jesus said. We don't have access to the Aramaic original. But the *Septuagint* almost always translates the Hebrew *nephesh* (נ פ ש) as *psyche* (ψυχή), and almost always the word *psyche* was used only to translate *nephesh*. Thus it is possible that Jesus said in Aramaic:

> For whoever wants to save his *nephesh* will lose it, but whoever loses his *nephesh* for me will find it.

Krister Stendahl told me, "Jeff, you should not say, 'it is possible that Jesus said in Aramaic . . . .' Instead you should say, 'There can be no doubt that Jesus used the Aramaic word *nephesh.*'" (Interview with Stendahl, July 29, 1993.)

"I don't understand," Rachel said. "Can you repeat the question?"

After I did, there was a long silence. Finally, she said:

"That feels like a Christian saying as opposed to a Jewish saying."

"What makes it Christian?" I asked. "Why isn't it Jewish?"

"Because this idea of succumbing to God is a Christian idea," she said. "The idea of passive submission to God's will is not Jewish. We emulate God. But we do so actively. We seek to be like God. But we don't submit ourselves to the will of God."

"What do you mean you 'seek to be like God'?" I asked.

"The more things you do and the more you study," she replied, "the more like God you become. I bristle at the idea of losing my soul for the sake of God. God has no interest in that."

"I find your comments profound," I said, "more profound than you think you are."

She giggled.

Chapter 4
Quenton Hyder, M.D.

When I first met Dr. Quenton Hyder, he was a mid-town Manhattan psychiatrist. His office was on West 44th Street. He also works at the Mental Health Center in Bridgeport, Connecticut. He is a born-again Christian. His evangelical, charismatic language is different than the way I think. I want to provide a variety of mental health points of view about the soul. Quenton strongly speaks for the fundamentalist, evangelical view.

1. Psychiatrists Treat the Soul

I asked Dr. Hyder whether he thinks that the *psyche* we treat in psychiatry is the biblical soul, or some part of the biblical soul.[7]

"Of course," he said. "I've been studying that for 20 to 30 years. As I see it, the soul is the totality of the personality. We can divide the personality into the thinking part and the feeling part. Either part can go wrong. When the thinking part goes wrong, the result is schizophrenia. When the feeling part goes wrong, the result is neurosis. There is also a spiritual dimension. The spirit, while not curative, does have a healing influence. I wouldn't go so far as to say that spirit or prayer can heal schizophrenia. But, of course, God could heal schizophrenia if He wanted to."

"Let me make sure I am understanding you," I said. "Are you saying that the personality is the soul?"

"Yes," he said. He talked fast, faster than I could write. "Now the soul is not all there is to a person. There is also the spiritual part. That is the part of us that is able to communicate with God. The soul isn't the part that communicates with God. And also there is the body. That is the part that dies. The spirit goes on after death into God's presence. The soul — well, I don't know what happens to the soul after death. But what you are discussing is the soul. That's not the spiritual part. The soul has a thinking process and a feeling process. I'd love to get together again for lunch to discuss this stuff with you. Let's get together for lunch."

I was delighted that he still thought so well of me.

"Well," I said, "I'm a bit busy now. Let me get back to you about that. When you divide the soul into thinking and feeling, where does bipolar disorder fit?"

"It's sort of a puzzle," he said. "Kind of fits both. I guess insofar as it is just a mood disorder, it is the feelings that went wrong. Insofar as it becomes psychotic, the thinking goes wrong. But I don't see much of that any more because lithium is so effective. Now you take major depression. According to *DSM-3R*, that would be the feelings that went wrong, providing it's not psychotic. Anyway, the soul is that part of us which is not anatomical and not physical. The unconverted, unsaved person has a soul, but his spirit would be inactivated. In other words, both the saved and the unsaved person have a soul. But the saved person has a spirit also."

"Do you use these ideas in your practice of psychiatry?" I asked. "For example, do you treat the spirit in addition to the soul?"

"Well, yes," he said. "Of course, you know that I have a very unusual practice. Eighty percent or more of my patients are Christians. That's because of the referral sources that I have. Most of my patients are referred from churches or Christian organizations."

I had come to appreciate something about Quenton when we last spoke, a couple of years ago. As strange as I found it for him to use a *King James Bible* in his practice of psychiatry, he is trusted by fundamentalist and evangelical ministers who don't trust any other psychiatrist. Therefore, he is able to help a whole constituency of people who otherwise would not receive psychiatric care. Born-again Christians and psychiatry are like oil and water. They don't mix. Except Quenton uses some kind of emulsifying agent so that they do mix.

"The patients know that I am an evangelical, born-again Christian before they walk through the door," Quenton continued. "So it's a tilted group of patients. There are a few pagans and a few Jews who come to me for help. And, of course, when I see a pagan, I don't mention any of this, because it would scare them off. But when I see a Christian, they expect me to discuss sin and morality, ethics, spirituality, and Jesus Christ. And I do. Listen, let's make a date and have lunch together and discuss this at greater length."

2. God's View of Our Soul

"Let me get back to you about lunch," I said. "Quenton, do you think that God's view of you can be known? Is there some way for you to access how God sees Quenton Hyder?"

"God reveals that to me daily," he said. "He requires me to be obedient to the thoughts that come into my mind during prayer and Bible reading."

On another occasion, Quenton had told me that God can and does control his thoughts, at least some of his thoughts. This time when I spoke with him I marveled at his use of the word "obedience." I have always wondered what Christians mean when they use this strange word. Here it seemed to mean "being receptive to and responsive to loose associations and primary process thinking."

"These thoughts that you are supposed to be obedient to," I said. "How do they differ from the loose associations that would be in the mind of someone you would call a pagan?"

"They may or may not be different," he said. "I've been at this for 45 years. Every day for 45 years I pray and I read the Bible. My experience over these years is that acting on these thoughts leads directly to decisions that lead directly to actions. You may question the authenticity of all this. I can't prove that it's authentic. But the results speak for themselves. It has worked — it has worked extremely well! After 45 years it hasn't failed once yet!"

He laughed.

3. Jesus' Paradox

"Jesus said," I commented, "that whoever seeks his *psyche* will lose it and who loses his *psyche* for Christ's sake will find it. The Greek word *psyche*, which is translated 'life,' might also be translated 'self' or 'soul.' Does that paradoxical saying have any meaning to you?"

"You mean the Greek word *psuche*?" Quenton asked.**

"Yes," I said. "Is that a saying that makes sense in your life?"

"Well, of course," he replied, "as a believing Christian. You have to understand that Christ was speaking to believers. He was telling them to give up all the pleasures of this world and their worldly goods and their mother and father. What he promised in exchange was both eternal life in Heaven, and also total fulfillment in this life. The more you surrender your will to Christ, the happier you are."

"What does this mean," I asked, "'surrender your will'? How do you find out what you are meant to do? How do you get your marching orders?"

"Through prayer," Quenton said.

"How exactly?" I asked.

"Well," he said, "when I pray I have ideas occur to me which I think is what God wants me to do. So I have a policy. I always wait 24 hours. That gives the Holy Spirit time to set me straight if I've made a mistake. Then I pray again the next day. And if I still think the same thing, that is what I am meant to do. I've been at this now 45 years and it works.

** Although Dr. Hyder spoke of *psuche*, the Greek word ψυχή can be represented in English either way, *psuche* or *psyche*. The Greek letter "υ" functioned both as the English "y" and the English "u," thus either *psuche* or *psyche* would be a correct translation. In this book I will follow the usual convention of writing *psyche*.

Nine times out of ten I get the right idea the first time. But I am an impetuous and hotheaded man, as all of us are, and so sometimes I get it wrong the first time. That's why the 24-hour wait is essential. I don't mean to say that I have lived a life free from sin. But I have tried to live a life under the leadership of the Holy Spirit. This, of course, is a specifically biblical evangelical way."

"There is a New Testament scholar named Krister Stendahl," I said, "who points out that this idea of self-denial and surrendering your will to Christ is not something that should be urged upon someone who is depressed, nor to someone whose self has been shattered by early childhood incest. What do you think of the idea of changing the message to fit the audience?"

"I agree with him," Quenton said. "That kind of challenge should not be given to someone who is mentally or physically fragile. A person must be mentally strong and physically healthy before you would tell them that to find their life they must be willing to lose it. That is why people who are quite competent and capable of making thousands of dollars a week forgo all that and become missionaries or some other work for the church which is not financially rewarding. But before you would challenge someone to forgo everything and surrender to Christ, you would first have to be talking to someone who is mentally healthy and physically strong, especially mentally healthy."

4. Child-like Core of Our Soul

"It seems to me that Freud condemned religion for encouraging a regressive child-like attitude," I said. "Yet I think there is a healthy child-like side to my religion. So I think that the correspondence between the child-like core of my soul, and my religion, proves the truth of what the theologians have always said. They said that God created us in such a way that God fulfills our deepest yearning and striving. What do you think?"

"I think the word we are skirting around here is 'dependency,'" Quenton said. "Psychiatrists tend to teach that being dependent is bad and that you should seek to be autonomous and self-determining. When I was trained in psychiatry at Columbia University, I constantly argued with my psychoanalytic colleagues about this. They were horrified that I said I was totally dependent on Christ. They thought I should outgrow it. They could respect only autonomy and self-determination. But I remain totally dependent on Christ even to this day. It is the healthiest lifestyle we can live. I think there is a philosophical diametrical opposition here. Freud taught that if you understand the problem, then you can pull yourself up by your bootstraps. But I interpret Scriptures to say that men are too proud to admit they have a need. We need God. If man in pride tries to live outside the Holy Spirit, that is simply prideful sin. The more I surrender my life to God, the more peace I have about going in the right direction. Surrender of the will is the key."

"Thank you for your help," I said.

"Let's get together for lunch," he said.

After our talk, I reflected on some of my differences with Dr. Hyder. He finds God speaking to him through his conscious thoughts and feelings. I find God speaking to me through my perplexity, unconscious, dreams, feelings, and cognitions.[8] Thus Dr. Hyder knows what God is telling him within 24 hours, whereas it sometimes takes me 24 years to sort out my confusion.

Chapter 5
Comment by Krister Stendahl

"You asked both Rachel and Dr. Quenton Hyder how God sees them," Stendahl said, "linked with the question how do they know how God sees them. What does that have to do with the idea of 'soul'? I don't see how you connect these things."

"This entire book starts," I replied, "with the statement I have heard from many biblical scholars, 'You don't **have** a soul, you **are** a soul.' From that statement I derive something like a working definition of the soul, namely 'Your soul is who you are.'"

"Yup," Stendahl replied. "That makes sense so far."

"Well," I continued, "the next step in my logic is to say that 'who you are' can be seen from two perspectives. On the one hand, perhaps you are the person you think you are. On the other hand, perhaps you are the person God thinks you are. Thus if your soul is who you are, and you are who God thinks you are, the question arises how you know who God thinks you are. Only if there is some access to God's thoughts about you could you know your soul."

"Yup," Stendahl replied. "Now I see how the idea of the soul is tied in to the idea of natural revelation or specific revelation: how a person knows what God thinks of them. That's OK. It makes sense. You remember that years ago I advised you to avoid trying to define the soul."

"Yes," I replied. "You said, 'You want to avoid reifying the word "soul." People will always be able to argue that you are wrong. The approach you take should be a creative one. You should create a modern idea of the soul, and then illustrate it with vivid and compelling passages from the Bible.'"

"Yes," he said, "that's right. But if you say the soul is your identity, is 'who you are,' you have avoided the pitfall because identity is not a thing, it cannot be reified."

Translation of *Psyche* (ψυχή)

"Krister," I said, "you have encouraged me in my non-standard translation of the verse:

> For those who want to save their *psyche* will lose it, but those who lose their *psyche* for my sake will find it (NRSV: Matthew 16:25, Mark 8:35, Luke 9:24, Luke 17:33, John 12:25).

"Most biblical scholars and most Bibles translate the Greek word *psyche* as 'life' in this verse. But in my book I want to quote that verse as saying:

> For those who want to save their **self** will lose it, but those who lose their **self** for my sake will find it.

"Or, alternatively:

> For those who want to save their **soul** will lose it, but those who lose their **soul** for my sake will find it."

"Of course, *psyche* means life in that verse," Stendahl replied, "but that translation doesn't exhaust the meaning of the verse. The Greek word *psyche* could be translated into English as 'soul,' 'life,' 'self,' 'psyche,' or 'I'. If the verse is translated,

> For those who want to save their **life** will lose it, but those who lose their **life** for me will find it,

then it almost limits itself to the idea of martyrdom. The more general self-denial meaning is not overt in that translation. The point is that there is no such thing as a perfect translation. There is always residual meaning, meaning which is not captured in the translation. There is an old saying, 'The translator is the traitor.' This is said because the original always means something more than is captured by any translation. Ultimately you cannot really translate anything from one language to another. There is even a question whether it is possible for one person to communicate what they mean to another person when talking in the same language. This is why, when someone talks about the meaning of the Bible, I always say, To whom? My point is that meaning is always in the context of persons. People use words to express what they mean."

"Your whole book, *Meanings*, is about that," I replied.[9] "What led me to think that the verse might be talking about self-denial is the context. The previous sentence is:

> If any want to become my followers, let them deny themselves and take up their cross and follow me (NRSV: Matthew 16:24; Mark 8:34)

"Then comes the verse about losing the *psyche* versus finding the *psyche*. Following that comes the verse which the *King James* translates:

> For what is a man profited, if he shall gain the whole world, and lose his own soul? or what shall a man give in exchange for his soul? (KJV: Matthew 16:26; Mark 8:36)

"When read in Greek the middle verse is not just talking about loss of life, but also loss of the self or soul, because the Greek word *psyche* could take on all those meanings. If a scholar thinks that Jesus were primarily thinking about martyrdom, then it might be translated 'life.' But if someone like me thinks that the Scriptures are psychologically sophisticated, then it might be translated 'self' or 'soul.'"

"What I want to do for you, Jeff, is write a proper preface for your book, in which I delve into the meaning of the word *psyche* in some depth," he continued. "But I would not be able to do that here on Nantucket. I would have to be at home in Cambridge where I would be able to consult books such as Kittel's *Theological Dictionary* and the *Septuagint Concordance*, and so on. The verse in question used the Greek word *psyche* instead of the other words meaning 'life,' such as *zōé* or *biōs*. My point is that the verse you quote would have had a different connotation if the Gospels said,

> For whoever wants to save his *zōé* will lose it, but whoever loses his *zōé* for me will find it.

"This is a tricky matter," Stendahl said, "and it will not be easy to convince Bible scholars that your ideas about this verse are correct. I don't want to leave you looking naive before the biblical experts. It would be a shame if they simply dismissed you by saying, 'This fellow Boyd is simply wrong about the translation of this verse.' Unfortunately, it will be many months before I can write a scholarly preface such as your book deserves."

The idea of my further imposing on this generous man troubled me. Stendahl is getting on in years, and has grown frail. His wife, Brita, when she spoke with me, indicated with her eyes and by her facial expression that I should go easy on Stendahl, not use up all the energy from his limited allotment.

I decided to decline Stendahl's offer to write what he considered a "proper preface" for this book, one that would stand up to the full force of scholarly skepticism.

Chapter 6
Dan Blazer, M.D., Ph.D.

Dr. Dan Blazer was interim chairman of psychiatry at Duke University Medical School. He was a leading contender for the chairmanship. Being uninterested in fulltime administration, he informed the search committee that he had no interest in becoming permanent chairman. I thought it was typical of Dan that he would not pursue the chairmanship because he was interested in a Kingdom that is not of this earth.

Six months later, however, I found Dan was dean of medical education at Duke, an administrative job he actually enjoys.

1. Psychiatrists Treat the Soul
I explained my concept that the "self" which we treat in psychiatry is 80% of the biblical "soul," but that the "soul" includes more than the "self" — especially that the "soul" includes our relationship with God, whereas the mental health concept of the "self" does not.[10]

"What you are saying makes a lot of sense to me," he said. "I believe there is a real vacuum in academic psychiatry. Mainstream psychiatry is missing something."

"What is missing?" I asked.

"The personality, the person," he said. "The need to seek for something more in life. What is missing is the motivation which will help patients to change because they are seeking for something. The spiritual restlessness which allows people to struggle in life is missing. Religious longing, craving, is missing. We are a people of the spirit. Psychiatry has become mechanistic. There is no longer any philosophy in psychiatry. On the other hand, your ideas are likely to be criticized because they are not typical, they are not the approved way of thinking."

"So you think that it makes sense to talk about a 'soul' which includes but surpasses the 'self'?" I reiterated.

"Yes, it does," he said. "I've struggled with how to put some of that together. My way of thinking about it is less elegant than your way of saying it. I was thinking along the lines of the Platonic division of a body, soul, and spirit. The soul in this way of thinking would be the personality. I taught an adult course at Bible school on this subject."

Wanting to hear what Dr. Blazer had to say, I bit my tongue about my objection to the body, soul, spirit way of thinking. My objection is that way of speaking leads many people to think of themselves as if they were divided by a Berlin Wall into three compartments. It would be as if the whole person could be fragmented the way our society is, into the part that the primary care doctor treats, the part that the psychotherapist treats, and the part which God treats. In the Bible it is clear that God laid claim on the whole person, not just the spiritual compartment.

"Bible school?" I asked. "What church do you belong to?"

"The Church of Christ," he said. "We're a small denomination in the South. Didn't you know I and my wife had been missionaries in Cameroon for a couple of years?"

"What kind of missionary?" I asked.

"Medical," he said. "I'm afraid it's a conservative religious background I come from."

"You know, you and I worked together for six years in the Epidemiologic Catchment Area Study," I said, "during the time when I worked for the National Institute of Mental Health. And I knew you were into religion. But you and I have never discussed religion before."

"What is really important in life doesn't get talked about in academic psychiatry," he said. "It gets buried."

"So you think the spiritual side of human life is crucial and not included in the mental health concept of the 'self?'" I asked.

"I would never think that psychiatric problems can be fixed by prayer," he said. "But on the other hand, psychiatry has neglected the spiritual side of the individual. We don't understand it nor do we use it very well. I speak sometimes of the 'quenched spirit.' Things have changed dramatically during my career in psychiatry. When I started out, psychoanalysis still had a big influence. There was a sense of antagonism between religion and psychiatry. That no longer exists. In the old days, psychoanalysts would sometimes feel embarrassed about their religion, or reject it. Other psychiatrists down here would convert and become evangelical Christians, and would reject psychiatry. The common theme was that religion and psychiatry were assumed to be incompatible. But over the decades all that has changed. People no longer talk about psychiatry and religion. It's not that they are incompatible, because no one today thinks they are incompatible. I've been astonished in my career how compatible they are. But people in major psychiatric training centers have stopped thinking about the big issues in life. Biological psychiatry is completely disconnected from faith. It is even disconnected from the 'self.'"

"It occurs to me," I said, "that the mental health movement can be divided in half. One half talks about the existence of the 'self' or the *psyche*, the other half doesn't. The 'self' or the *psyche*, of course, is the 'soul' in disguise — the earthly aspect of the soul. But biological psychiatry doesn't even believe in the *psyche*."

"You're right," Dan said. "Morton Reiser published an article on that subject back ten years ago. It was called 'Is Psychiatry Losing Its Mind?'[11] It was the lead article in the *American Journal of Psychiatry*. The trouble is today psychiatrists are taking the attitude that they don't want to think about that. You see a lot of that in life. Psychiatrists don't want to think about the larger issues of life, doctors don't want to think about the rising cost of health care, and nobody wants to think about the economic problems of our nation." (We spoke before the 1992 presidential race when Bill Clinton, Ross Perot, and George Bush debated such issues.)

"Does your religious side play a role in your work at Duke?" I asked.

"I never initiate biblical concepts in therapy," he said. "But patients generally know that this is important to me. So it becomes part of the assumptions that a patient and I share. Like a patient will say, 'God is helping me through this,' and I will say, 'I know what you mean.' My faith has driven me to be the best psychiatrist that I can. I've wanted to stay in academia."

"Why?" I asked.

"Because that's where the cutting edge is in psychiatry," Dan said. "I've always felt that it was important for me as a Christian to be in academia, visible. I have not been that ambitious. The acting chairmanship was thrust on me against my resistance. What I have wanted is to have my colleagues respect me. When my colleagues see me they observe that my faith is not a weakness, nor is it a drawback to being a good psychiatrist. Generally, I think I am respected as being the best psychiatrist I can be. It is astounding that I have found so little conflict between psychiatry and religion. What I love is clinical care and teaching and research. I hate administration. That's why I turned down the fulltime chairmanship when the dean tried to interest me in it."

2. God's View of Our Soul

"Dan," I said, "I have a different question. If you can imagine that God sees Dan Blazer, is there some way for you to gain access to God's view of you?"

There was a silence.

"I have never really thought about that," he said. "You've given me something to think about that I never before thought about. There's no question He knows me as a specific personality. I believe God knows me perfectly. But I have not felt any compelling need for me to figure out what God's view of me is. To the degree that I can understand myself more perfectly, I am getting closer to what God knows. I don't spend a lot of time worrying what God thinks of me. My effort is focused on trying to understand myself."

"Some people speak of God leading them," I suggested, gently.

"I feel strongly that God leads me," he affirmed, "through Scriptures. There's a drawing power to God. Christian life is a journey toward perfection. I reverberate to the idea of a Pilgrim's Progress, with God leading. In the Scriptures it speaks of The Way."

"I thought that God might know me even better than my analyst," I suggested.

"I've never been in psychoanalysis," he said. "But I imagine the patient worries about what the analyst is thinking, and wants to change the analyst's mind about the patient. The analyst is human. So it's quite different when I speak of God. God already knows me perfectly. So God is different than an analyst. The pressure is off, because God already knows me perfectly, so I don't have to put any effort into changing God's mind about me. For me the important issue is not whether God knows me, but whether I know God, whether I know His Will perfecting me."

"What specifically do you mean by 'His Will?'" I asked. "How do you operationalize that?"

"Life is a journey, a searching," Dan said. "It is important to me to walk in the way of the Lord. Not that there is just one way. But on the other hand, I can't just go my own way either, I can't just say 'Whatever fits me, I'll do.' So I think that I can't find the path simply by doing what feels right to me. That sense of looking solely inside for meaning wears thin very fast — it leads nowhere. The source of meaning has to be external to me. So there is a path for me to follow, but it is not just one rigid path, it is flexible. But it is a path leading to perfection."

"In summary," I ventured, "when I asked whether God's view of you can be known, you replied that God knows

you perfectly, and leads you on a journey toward perfection."
"Exactly," he said.

3. A Paradox About the Soul

I asked Dan what he thought of the paradox that to seek one's soul or self is to lose it, and to lose it for Christ's sake is to find it. I conceded that the Greek word *psyche* is often translated "life" in this paradox.

"I have never thought of it that way," Dan said. "I don't get it."

"Well, what does the saying mean to you?" I felt frustrated.

"I guess I always thought it meant losing your life," Dan replied.

"You mean martyrdom?" I asked.

"Yeah," he said, "Martyrdom. Sacrificial life."

"When you say 'sacrificial life' you aren't just referring to death," I said, relieved to get beyond the impasse. "You are speaking of losing the 'self' in everyday life."

"Not death," he said. "Sacrificial life means giving yourself for others. The goal of life is not finding your identity."

"Doesn't that contradict some aspects of psychotherapy?" I asked. "Does Christ call us to lose the identity we find through psychotherapy?"

"No, it's not a contradiction," Dan said. "Your humanistic identity would be lost. You would put on the identity of the sacrificial self."

"What do you mean, 'the sacrificial self?'" I asked.

"I think it is in Philippians where Paul talks about taking on the attitude of Christ as a servant," he said.

The passage reads:

Let the same mind be in you that was in Christ Jesus, who . . . emptied himself, taking the form of a slave . . . he humbled himself and became obedient to the point of death — even death on a cross. (NRSV: Philippians 2:5-8)

"As I understand the Christian faith," Dan said, "one doesn't become Jesus, but one takes on those characteristics.

Jesus is a model. And the specific characteristics are those of a servant and the sacrificial self."

"Is that how you live, Dan?" I asked.

"I try," he said. "Sometimes, often, I fall short of the goal. I don't know if I live that way. But I would like to. That's my goal. It means a life of service. My son graduated from Duke University today. He's going into environmental management. And Marian Wright Edelman was the commencement speaker. You know her?"

"She runs the Children's Defense Fund," I said, "in Washington, D.C."

"That's right," Dan said. "Well, she was telling the graduates that they should seek a life of service. 'Service is the price you pay for living,' she said.[12] So there is an example of a service-oriented movement in the world."

"But the mental health movement is not the origin of these ideas about serving others," I said. "The mental health movement has an enormous influence in America today. And it is popularly understood as urging self-actualization or fulfilling your potential. I challenge you to cite any example of the mental health movement in America today telling people they will find themselves only by losing themselves in service to others."

"You are right," he said. "The mental health movement is not the source of these ideas about service."

"Your comments about service and the sacrificial self," I said, "remind me of a comment by Krister Stendahl, a New Testament professor. He says that one should not preach service and self-sacrifice to people who are depressed, nor to patients who have no 'self' because of incest or child abuse leaving them damaged in their core. What do you think of that idea?"

"Faith is a matter of stages," Dan replied. "It would be pathological to start out at stage one by saying that Christianity requires self-sacrifice. That isn't the first stage. The initial response to Christianity is always, 'I can't believe what Christ has done for me!' A Christian says, 'I'm really nothing without Christ. It doesn't matter whether I have been highly successful, or whether I have been a failure in the world. I am nothing without Christ. But in Christ I can do all things. I have an incomparable life in Christ.' Whether your life is easy or whether it is tough, this is the natural response to grace. So that is the first stage.

"Only when one feels that way does one begin to think about a sacrificial life," Dan continued. "The desire to give arises naturally out of the experience of being grateful. So I agree with Professor Stendahl."

4. Child-like Core of Our Soul

I explained my idea that Freud's observation about the regressive nature of religion could be turned on its head, and used as proof that God has so created us that God fulfills the yearnings of our soul.

"I think Freud was more religious than he appeared to be," said Dan. "Hans Küng's book on Freud showed this."[13]

"Thank you for talking with me," I said.

Months later I received this letter from Dan:

"Dear Jeff:

"I have had an opportunity to review the draft of your book. I found it *very interesting*. You have stimulated my thinking about these issues. I believe that you are on the right track.

"I believe cognitive therapy is influencing psychiatry much more than psychoanalytic theory today. One reason may be that psychiatry has become increasingly empirical and 'biologic' and therefore, as we discussed, the issue of God (or lack thereof) has been ignored rather than debated.

"Sincerely, Dan
"J. P. Gibbons Professor of Psychiatry"

Chapter 7
Sally

Sally is a psychiatrist who prefers that her real name not be used.

Sally wanted to clarify that her comments were off the cuff, and in the spirit of brainstorming. Apparently, I caught her off guard by phoning to say I wanted to interview her. She says that my quoting our telephone interview verbatim encouraged her to "shoot from the hip" and say things that she would not normally want to put in print. She says this chapter does not accurately represent how she might have responded had she been approached in a different manner. She was kind of uncomfortable that I wrote down exactly what she said during the interview. But she said that, "With that addition, I would be comfortable with your publishing the chapter. I think what you are doing is important. We serve the same Lord, and advancing the cause of Christ is the most important issue here."[14]

1. Psychiatrists Treat the Soul

I explained to her the nature of my book, and the thesis that the *psyche* that we treat in psychiatry is the biblical soul, but that the soul is even larger than the *psyche*.

"I am much more comfortable with the word *psyche* than the word 'soul,'" she said, "but I agree with what you are saying. I would not think there is anything particularly religious about the soul, or *psyche*, any more than there is anything religious about the body. The 'soul' would not be rejected in psychiatric circles, if you explained that it is actually the *psyche*. I think of a person as being made up of the soma, the *psyche*, and the spirit. Of course, you can't divide a person into parts. It is the spirit which is ignored these days. That is what is missing from psychiatry. The spirit is what I am concerned about."

"How does this way of thinking affect your work as a psychiatrist?" I asked.

"Well, I think there are certain kinds of pathology that are ignored by modern psychiatry," she said.

"Like what?" I asked.

"Like anger and lack of forgiveness," Sally replied. "Someone can become bitter and emotionally hard because they don't forgive someone else. We don't have a framework for discussing that problem in psychiatry. We talk with a patient about their feelings, but there is no psychiatric concept of forgiveness. The theologians talk about it."

"What do the theologians say?" I asked.

"That lack of forgiveness leads to resentment," she said, "and retards healing. It can be overcome by confession."

I have been talking with mental health professionals for years now, in preparation for writing this book. A recurrent theme has been the absence of a concept of forgiveness in the mental health field. Therapists who are faithful often see this as a void in mental health theory.

"Actually," I said, "I want to go back to something you said earlier. I think of the soul as being larger than the *psyche*. If you think of me as being defined by the different intimate emotional relationships that I form, my relationship with my spouse, my children, workers, and parents, would all be part of my *psyche*. However, my relationship with God would not be part of my *psyche*. That's why the soul is larger than the *psyche*."

"Yeah," she said, "but I tend to think of that as the spirit. There are two kinds of spirit. There is the spirit which is external, and there is also an internal spirit which is part of us. I've been excited by the book of Rudolph Otto called *The*

Idea of the Holy. He talks about the religious feeling, the sense of awe, the *mysterium tremendum.* In a religious experience the *psyche* and spirit are all merged. And it has a very healing effect, this experience of transcendence. A good example is Alcoholics Anonymous, which uses the spirit for a healing purpose."

"I was at an open AA meeting yesterday," I said. "Not that I am an alcoholic. Just as an observer."

"Most physicians have never been to an AA meeting," Sally said. "They don't realize that God is part of it, that AA uses a spiritual approach. Which is necessary because there is a bad spiritual aspect to alcoholism. That's why psychiatrists are not successful in treating alcoholism. There is a spiritual dimension to other diseases also.

"I just treated a woman with Post Traumatic Stress Disorder," she continued. "A drunken teenager had smashed his car into hers. Her PTSD symptoms lingered, and we discovered that she was having trouble forgiving this kid. Of course, there were other things going on also. She was a person who needed to be in control and in charge, and the accident left her feeling not in control. But one piece of it was forgiveness.

"I don't think that sin is the basis of every distress. Not all disorders come from spiritual causes. It is a knotty problem. We have to think of a balance. Not all mental distress is sin, but some is. Mental illness is not all from the mental side, not all from the *psyche.* All healing doesn't come from prayer and spiritual approaches, but some does.

"The most untreatable people I see in the field of geriatrics," Sally continued, "are the ones with no religion. They are people with existential despair, what Victor Frankl calls a loss of meaning. I can't send them to church because they aren't interested. Psychiatry has nothing to offer them."

2. God's View of Our Soul

"I have another question," I said.

"Only one more?" she replied.

"Well, it is true that there is a problem containing this material and putting limits on it," I said. "One question seems to lead to ten others. My question is this: If God has a view of Sally, is that something that you can know or gain access to?"

"What would make you ask a question like that?" she asked.

"Well, one of my ideas about the soul," I said, "is that it refers to the person God sees when God looks at me. You know, I was in psychoanalysis. I felt profoundly known by my analyst. It occurs to me that God must know me at least that well."

"Oh yes," she said, "yes."

"In my book I define 'Your soul is who you are.' But who are you? There are at least two ways to look at it: that you are who you think you are, or that you are who God thinks you are. If the soul were defined as who God thinks you are, the problem with that definition is that someone might say, 'How are you to know how God sees you, Dr. Boyd?' So that's why I ask the question."

"My answer is, 'Ideally yes,'" Sally replied, "'but because of sin we keep ourselves at arm's length from knowing the depth of His love.'

"We might not be able to take it," Sally continued. "It might be an overwhelming experience to know how deeply we are loved. Your experience of being known by another is my experience, too. It is such a powerful experience. The Scripture verse that comes to mind is:

> For now we see in a mirror, dimly, but then we will see face to face. Now I know only in part; then I will know fully, even as I have been fully known. (NRSV: 1 Corinthians 13:12)

"I found that my relationship with my analyst wasn't so one-sided," Sally said. "Of course, I never learned all kinds of practical details about his life. But there was a mutuality to the way in which my analyst and I knew one another. We interacted. Our work together was like a joint creation."

"In my case," I said, "I came to know how my analyst would respond when I brought up certain feelings. And that is what I internalized. That responsiveness of my analyst became internal — it became part of what I took away after the analysis had ended."

"Yes," Sally said. "And I think we internalize our relationship with God or Christ. Of course, for us to fully know Christ we will have to wait until we see Him face to face. Meanwhile, we know only in part, through supernatural means such as worship or the Holy Spirit."

3. A Paradox

I explained my favorite paradox about seeking versus losing one's life, *psyche*, self, soul. "Does that make sense to you?" I asked.

"There are a lot of paradoxes in faith," Sally said. "For example, the general perception is that faith means abdication of responsibility. Like a patient with massive skin burns is expected to be passive and resigned if he has faith. Yet the data contradict this expectation. The data show that the more faith one has the more active the person is. Research has shown that the medical symptoms which a patient prays about are most likely those symptoms which the person has spoken to a physician about.

"Faith is full of paradoxes," she continued. "God is supposed to be in control of everything, yet people of faith are more active in trying to be responsible for their lives, rather than less active. People outside the faith don't understand this paradox. The Catholic Church and the black church have been criticized for fostering passivity and helplessness, and allowing powerful authority figures to make all the decisions. To outsiders what looks like abdicating responsibility isn't that at all.

"This doesn't directly relate to the paradox you mentioned, Jeff," Sally said, "but it illustrates the importance of paradox in our faith. By the way, how did you happen to get interested in that particular paradox?"

"I was writing a book on the soul," I replied, "so I grew interested in the Greek word *psyche*. Most times when *psyche* is used in the New Testament it is not translated 'soul.' But I was interested in what it would mean if we kept in mind that 'soul' is one possible translation. This particular paradox about seeking and losing your *psyche* was repeated many times in the New Testament."

4. Child-like Core of Our Soul

"Another question I want to ask," I said, "concerns the appeal of our religion to the child-like core of our soul. Psychologists tell us that the core of our soul was established in infancy, and theologians tell us that our religion fulfills the core of our soul. It seems to me that some of the healthy child-like and regressive yearnings of my soul are fulfilled by my religion. Being child-like is the key to fearlessness, playfulness, creativity, trust, openness, folderol, and astonishment. For example, my own relationship with God is one of trust and occasionally letting down my boundaries, the same way I related to my mother when I was an infant. What do you think of that?"

"Mary as a mother figure would be what I would think of," Sally said.

"Tell me more," I said.

"Being a convert to Catholicism," she said, "I have been trying to learn about the Catholic faith. The saints are similar to friends whom one might ask, 'Could you pray for me about this?' Just because your friend happens to be dead, still you can ask the friend to pray for you. And Mary is like the ultimate saint in this regard, because of her mothering qualities."

"What mothering qualities?" I asked.

"There are hundreds of traditions about Mary," Sally said.

"Yes," I said, "but I am interested in you. What is your relationship with Mary like?"

"Mary is the epitome of the friends that intercede for you. Some friends I ask more frequently than others, 'Will you pray for me?' Mary is the epitome of all that because she is trustworthy, compassionate, very powerful — the Queen of Heaven — and also humble, and devoted to carrying out the will of her Son."

"Hmmm," I said. "Can you compare and contrast your relationship with your mother to your relationship with Mary?"

"I am closer to Mary than to my mother," she said. "There is a deeper knowing. Some friends know me better than my family knows me, and Mary is such a friend. That's why people make up affectionate names for Mary to help evoke fond memories, the way one makes up affectionate names for someone you love."

"Like what?" I asked.

"Our Lady of the Holy Rosary, Our Lady of Sorrows, Our Lady of Guadalupe," she said. "These names are often used in a litany."

"Thank you for sharing all that with me," I said.

So being affectionately desirous of you, we were willing to have imparted unto you, not the gospel of God only, but also our own **souls**, because ye were dear unto us.

(KJV: 1 Thessalonians 2:8)

So deeply do we care for you that we are determined to share with you not only the gospel of God but also our own **selves**, because you have become very dear to us.

(NRSV: 1 Thessalonians 2:8)

Chapter 8
Susan Leigh Deppe, M.D.

Dr. Sue Deppe is a clinical instructor in the psychopharmacology and geriatric service of the University of Vermont College of Medicine, where she sees patients and does research on geriatric depression. She has a private practice in adult psychiatry, with a particular interest in mood disorders, women's issues, and spirituality. Sue has lectured to professional, clergy, and community groups on a range of topics including depression, mental health and spiritual growth. She is a certified lay speaker in the United Methodist Church and a member of several dialogue groups of clergy and mental health professionals. She and her husband are in a ministry of music throughout Vermont, northern New York, and their local faith community.

I explained the nature of my investigation.[15]

1. Psychiatrists Treat the Soul
"It makes sense that the 'self' or *psyche* is the 'soul,'" she said, "but I don't have the theological qualifications to feel sure about that. What is the soul? How are you defining it?"

"I will answer that," I said. "But first I want to find out what you think. What is the *psyche* or 'self' in your opinion?"

"Well, in my personal experience, and in my work with patients, work on psychological issues goes hand in hand with work on spiritual issues. People struggle with both, whether they are aware of it or not. In clinical practice, as much as we would like to keep psychological and spiritual issues separated, they are linked. Of course, I don't know what the theologians would say."

"Theologians today," I said, "seem to have little to say about the soul. In the Bible the soul was a person's breath. It was the living, vibrant part of a person, including the person's emotions such as anxiety and depression. It included the person's ability to relate to other people. Probably the closest phrase we have in English would be 'true identity' or 'self.' Your soul is who you are."

"If that is true, then psychiatrists are very involved with the soul. So the soul is what made a person unique?" she asked.

"Yes," I said.

"Well, we are just looking at different facets of the same thing. Is the soul what God or the spirit works on?" she asked. "I think of the mind, emotions, personality, cognition. But there is also a spiritual component of a person."

"Is that your experience?" I asked.

"Yes," she said. "I believe that we are spiritual creatures. But I don't think the soul is necessarily separate. All parts of ourselves are involved in interacting with God."

2. God's View of Our Soul

"Another question," I said. "Is God's view of Susan Deppe knowable? Is that way of seeing you something you can gain access to?"

"It would feel presumptuous to think so," she said. "I think we can know what God can do with people in general. Of course, if we give up control, then we can let God walk with us. We can figure out what God wants us to be and to do. If I were not a person of faith, then I would say this is just wishful thinking. But I am a person of faith. I think God does lead, if we just get out of the way enough. God has work for us to do.

"Tell me about yourself," she said. "How did you get into this research project?"

I told her my background. "I am chairman of psychiatry at a general hospital," I said. "I work full time as a psychiatrist treating the *psyche* or 'self.' And sometimes on weekends I lead worship services and minister to the 'soul,' for I am also an ordained minister. So I am trying to write a book to prove to myself that I am one person and not two."

"Boy, can I relate to that conflict," she said. "For a long time I kept trying to figure out whether to believe in God or in psychiatry. My pastor suggested several books to read: Weatherhead's *The Will of God*, Phillips' *Your God Is Too Small*, Rabbi Harold Kushner's *When Bad Things Happen to Good People*, John Sanford, Morton Kelsey, and so on. When I got my hands on Kelsey's *Encounter With God*, it dawned on me that this didn't have to be an either-or proposition. I could have both. Peck's book *The Road Less Traveled* was wonderful. It was like he was saying things I had known all my life but never articulated.[16]

"I really struggle with the boundary issues, though. I am very careful to be respectful with patients. I don't think psychiatrists or therapists should push their religion. I cringe when I hear about colleagues who try to convert a patient, which is a blatant abuse of the therapist's power.[17] There are so many people who have been damaged by organized religion, or abused in the name of religion. It is not surprising to me that many people want nothing to do with the church. But it is sad. I think they throw the baby out with the bath water. And they lose a community that was the basis of society a few generations ago and that, if healthy, can provide a lot of social support now. One of my favorite clergymen has referred to the church and its small groups as an excellent holding environment. We have seen that in our congregation."

"What denomination are you?" I asked.

"United Methodist," she said.

"Yet you are a born again Christian?" I asked.

"Yes," she said, "I am in a mainline denomination. Yet I have been born again. The Holy Spirit is alive and well in the United Methodist Church. Hopefully, the United Methodist Church is alive in the Spirit as well. But I am a person who respects the boundaries of my profession. I do not use my psychiatric practice to proselytize. I try to help patients to explore *their* faith, question *their* framework of meaning, and become healthier. Sometimes that means they need to challenge some assumptions they have made. I do a lot of evangelism through music on the weekends. That does not mean God is absent from my office, however."

3. Jesus' Paradox

"I want to ask a different question," I said. "The Gospels quote Jesus as saying that if you want to save your life you will lose it, while if you are willing to lose it for Jesus' sake, you will save it or find it. The word which is translated 'life' can also be translated 'self.'"

"Yes," she said.

"So," I asked, "what does that paradox mean in the context of your life?"

"I am not an expert on these matters," Sue said. "I find this paradox to be very rich. I think it has to do with surrendering ourselves to the will of God. To put it bluntly, if we live for ourselves without a connection to the greater meaning of life, we lose. But if I take myself out of the way, then my life becomes richer. Jesus made it pretty clear that is what we are supposed to do."

"There is a New Testament professor named Krister Stendahl," I said.

"I've heard of him," she replied.

"He says that we have to be careful when we quote a paradox such as this," I said. "Stendahl says it might be OK to talk about that idea to someone like yourself or me, who is in reasonably good shape psychologically. But he points out that you have to tailor the Scripture to fit the audience. You wouldn't want to talk about loss of the 'self,' Stendahl says, to someone who is severely depressed, or who has no sense of 'self' to begin with. What do you think of that idea?"

"I agree with Stendahl," Sue said. "There are certain Scriptures I would not focus on with someone who was depressed. There are others I won't point out to a patient with a history of severe abuse, and others I would avoid with paranoid patients. It is a question of what we emphasize, where we focus. Psalm 27 is a beautiful psalm for some persons who have suffered severe abuse.[18] I might remind depressed patients about Jesus' forgiveness, or ask them about Jesus' love of even the unacceptable people and those who have failed. Jesus' interaction with Peter is a wonderful story most of us can relate to.[19] Peter denied Jesus three times — he was so very human — and then Jesus came back after the resurrection and gave Peter another chance to pledge his love. Peter, forgiven, became the rock on which the church was built.

"Actually, I don't quote Scripture often. If a patient refers to it, I try to understand its dynamic and real meaning for him or her. Religious material can be explored and interpreted psychodynamically. If necessary, I offer patients alternative ways of looking at things or point out images, for example, some of the beautiful female images in the Bible.[20] I am pretty clear with patients that I am not seminary-trained. I encourage people to get support from clergy who will not lay a guilt trip on them."

4. The Child-Like Core of Our Soul

"Here is another question," I said.

"Ask on," she said enthusiastically.

"Sigmund Freud said that religion so closely corresponds to what we really want in life that it must be an infantile wish-fulfillment projection. Yet Freud also admitted that he had no way of saying what is real and what is not real. Like he admitted he could not say whether God is real."

"There has been long-standing debate in the psychoanalytic literature about the existence of God," Sue responded. "In a 1975 article in the *Canadian Psychiatric Association Journal*, psychiatrist M.O. Vincent had this to say: 'The question of God's existence cannot be approached through conclusions drawn from the study of human personality.'"[21]

"I think we can take Freud's argument and turn it upside down," I said. "Theologians have always said that God has constructed us in such a way that our deepest yearnings are toward God. And that is precisely what Freud was describing, that a person's deepest yearnings are toward God. Like the yearning to have an omnipotent Parent who takes care of you. What do you think of that idea?"

"I believe that God uses science and biology," Sue said. "I can't really see it any other way. I don't think our biology is all random. But on the other hand, the question you raise is a disturbing one. It is disturbing because it raises the question of whether our needs are such that religion is simply a fiction to meet our needs. But what it comes down to is whether God is real or not. Ever since 1986, I have been convinced that God is real.

"Our parents and other important people have a profound impact on our images of God," Sue said. "It can take some work to sort out parents from God, especially if a patient has been abused by parents or the church.

"I think there is a lot more to religion than we see in Freud's observation," Sue continued. "My faith also involves worship and praise of God: not only asking for things, but recognizing who God is, praising God, and asking what God wishes me to do. Who are the models of mature faith in the Judeo-Christian tradition, or any other tradition? They are people who have placed themselves in God's will and love others deeply and sacrificially.

"A central aspect of my faith," Sue continued, "is the need to take myself out of the way. I have to remove my own selfish viewpoint, my laziness, apathy, so that it is not such an obstacle between me and God. I am not talking like Calvin, saying I am a worm. I am influenced mostly by Wesley, who said that we are going on toward perfection."

"Do you find that your basic yearning, psychologically, is for God?" I asked.

"Yes," Sue replied. "This is what drives the journey of faith for me: the desire to be in relationship. The other deep need is for community. I am very grateful that Christianity is meant to be lived out in community."

Chapter 9
David Larson, M.D., M.S.P.H.

David Larson is a psychiatrist who had been at the National Institute of Mental Health (NIMH) when I was there. In those days, I admired his courage because he was willing to be forthright about publishing research articles on religion and mental health. I was more embarrassed about Jesus in those days, and wanted to keep my lantern hidden beneath a bushel basket, although I did co-author one paper with him.[22] David also seemed insecure and somewhat apologetic on a personal level in the early 1980s when we worked together.

At the time of this interview, David still worked for the federal government, but at a much higher level. He works in the office of the secretary of the Department of Health and Human Services, doing health care planning and policy evaluation for the entire United States. As I write, David is moving to the Office of Alternative Medicine, which is part of the director of the National Institutes of Health's office.

Whereas he used to squeak like a mouse, now he roars like a lion. The feeling of neurosis and insecurity that I encountered in the past with him is now gone. There is a new sense of self-assurance, and an ebullience that is refreshing. His exuberant viewpoint is evident in the new book he wrote with his wife, *The Forgotten Factor in Physical and Mental Health: What Does the Research Show?*[23] The "forgotten factor" is religion.

1. Psychiatrists Treat the Soul

I explained my notion that there is a biblical soul, which includes the self or *psyche* of mental health.[24]

"You are on to something, Jeff," David said. "Go for it. Carl Jung once said that what brings about a cure in patients is their religion. And that is what we are finding in our research. It is important to struggle with that aspect of a patient. Ernest Becker said the same thing in *Denial of Death*.[25] He said we have to struggle with that aspect of the patient which is immortal, have to work on spiritual well-being. But this aspect of mental health is almost totally ignored by the mental health field (except for pastoral counselors and chaplains). Oskar Pfister was ignored. Mental health professionals simply ignore the most important aspect. Why? Consider the apostasy rate. Twenty-five percent of mental health professionals have turned out of their faith. This includes psychiatrists, psychologists, and social workers in mental health."[26]

Apostasy was such an archaic word! It stuck in my ear with a medieval ring.

"What do you mean, 'turned out of their faith'?" I asked.

"They abandoned the faith they were raised in," David explained. "'Apostasy' was the word the researchers used."

"And 25% is higher than the United States general population?" I asked, astonished.

"Much higher," David said. "The apostasy rate is 40% for someone going through psychoanalytic training. For those mental health professionals who never had any personal therapy, the apostasy rate is much lower. The anti-God influence seems to be part of the educational process of personal therapy: 'We got to do something about your religion neurosis.' But it is also a matter of peer pressure. I call it the 'anti-tenure variable.'"

What did he say?

"Anti-tenure variable?" I asked.

"You know," he said, "the variable that lowers your opportunity of getting tenure in academia."

I roared with laughter. When David and I had worked at NIMH, it was fear of not getting tenure at some university which had led me to hide my priesthood under a bushel basket. That fear had led me to avoid like leprosy the idea of writing this book. Something that Darrel Regier recently said to me confirmed my worries about David ever getting tenure in academia.

"You want to ruin your chances of ever getting tenure," David laughed. "Just do it. Just publish a paper in this area! 'He published what?' the promotions committee would say. The federal government is more tolerant of religion than are medical school promotions committees. If you are climbing through the ranks of academia, forget it! You will ruin your chances of ever getting tenure in mental health if you touch religion as a research variable."

"I used to be embarrassed about Jesus," I said, embarrassed about myself. "In some ways I feel freer to be more intellectually honest now that I am speaking honestly."

"Well, I still get scared about this," David said. "A sense of humor helps. People can tolerate me more easily because I can laugh at myself. But I was scared shitless in the beginning. I was afraid researching religion would really shatter my possible research career."

Having been trained in the civil rights movement, I detected the subtle effect of discrimination on the self-image of the oppressed. Over the decades I have come to believe that the only way for a minority-group member to feel self-respect is to refuse to accept the discrimination. David and I are minority-group members in the mental health field.

"From early training we learn of the need to deal with unresolved emotional issues," David continued. "Therapists often have unresolved feelings about religion or religious issues. When I present research data about religion to a mental health audience, I point out that the data are asymmetrical. About 75 to 80% of the time religion is beneficial to health. About 10% of the time it is neutral. And about 10% of the time it is harmful. Mental health audiences react with surprise. They are stunned. It isn't what they expect of religion as an independent variable in mental health research."

I asked, "What do you think of this idea that there is a soul, which is the whole person, and that what we treat in the mental health field is but one aspect of that soul — the earthly aspect if you will?"

"You are on target, Jeff," he reiterated. "It's like Woody Allen's 'orgasmatron box.' Ernest Becker said there is something in us that lives forever. We have got to deal with that aspect of patients which goes on and on and on, something that exists beyond the reductionism of the modern age. My colleagues and I have demonstrated in our publications that religion helps as a health-care variable. You know the epidemiologic research methods that you and I use, Jeff, do not require that the usual boring variables be used as independent variables."

"You are saying," I asked, "that mental health can be the outcome variable, and religion can be one of the independent variables in epidemiologic research?"

"Absolutely," David said. "In most research about health it turns out that religion helps.[27] It seems to help as frequently as psychotherapy. The effect of religion on mental health is more powerful than any mental health therapy. It is cheap! It is effective! And it is plentifully available!"

Suddenly I understood how an odd duck like David could survive as a health care planner for the United States government. He was studying a variable that had a powerful effect on the health of Americans. I could imagine him convincing people that this variable had tremendous power in the prevention of illness and coping with illness. It was a variable that could not only empower but reduce the cost of health care, I imagined.

"Religion has a surprising effect on prevention," he said, "in research studies. It has preventive benefit. It has emerged in the stress research as a way of helping people cope with stress.[28] Yet the mental health researchers either don't study it, or study it inadequately. The religion variable often pops up from the data as the most powerful variable, and the people publishing the research never even discuss it. I showed this in my 'systematic review' paper."

Further details of Dr. Larson's thinking about this can be found at the end of this chapter.

2. God's View of Our Soul

"David," I said, "I want to ask you a different question. Do you think that God's view of you is accessible? Is there some way for you to know how God sees you, who you are?"

"Yes," he replied. "It has changed me during the years you have known me, Jeff."

"God's view of you has had an impact on you?" I asked, fascinated.

"God loves me," he said. "That is what I keep finding. There is hardly any negative shit. I would have expected more criticism. But there isn't. It is almost entirely positive, like a huge pillow of love."

"Yes but," I asked, "how has that had an impact on you?"

"It has made me immensely more self-confident," he said. "I am much more willing to be honest. And I have learned that I can be openly angry without it killing me. Angry and impatient. Because that is who I am. I can be an angry bastard. I've been listening to the minor prophets on audio cassettes when I drive to work. It dawned on me that God was very angry. Angry but fair. So I said to myself, 'If God can do it, then why can't I?' I get murderously angry these days. When you knew me at NIMH, I was always anxious."

He certainly was.

"And that is what all that anxiety was about," David continued. "I was anxious lest my anger or my impatience get expressed. I was filled with anxiety. But now most of the feared anxiety is gone. Now I feel able to express my anger and be done with it."

"I see what you are saying," I said. "I get anxious with this book I am writing. You must have been anxious when you started publishing all those research articles on religion and mental health."

"God might reject it," he said. "That was my biggest anxiety. I might go to all this effort to write an article and publish it at great personal academic risk, and God wouldn't like it. You might have some of that anxiety. That God might reject what you write."

The light bulb went on inside my brain. I suddenly understood a strange anxiety that had been haunting me as I wrote this book. Perhaps after twenty-five years of work, God would say I had produced something worthless. I also was anxious because a respectable professional like me is not supposed to talk openly about faith. Not only do psychiatrists not do it. Episcopalians don't do it. We're too genteel. I figured that David was some kind of Southern Baptist or Pentecostal that could get away with talking about God without embarrassment, whereas we Episcopalians had more of a sense of social propriety.

"What church do you go to?" I asked him.

"The Episcopal Church," David said.

"We love it because the Episcopalians really know how to worship," David continued. "I'm tired of these unstructured worship environments. I grew up in unstructured worship environments, and I'm tired of it. When you get to be my age and a professional like me, I mean, hey, you deserve to go to church and regress — just sit there like a child. When I go to church I just want to worship God. None of this other stuff. All I want to do is get into worshipping God. And, you know, that's what I feel in the Episcopal Church."

3. A Paradox About the Soul

"I am interested in a paradox about the soul," I said, "that if you seek it you will lose it, but if you are willing to lose it for Jesus' sake, you will find it. What do you think of that?"

"I have fallen in love with the paradoxes in Scripture," David said. "My favorite one is when they bring to Jesus the woman caught in the act of adultery. Do you remember the first paradoxical thing Jesus did?"

"He bent down and wrote in the sand with his finger," I said.

"Exactly," David said. "Playing in the dirt was a powerful statement. It makes the demands less important. It meant the bad guys had to wait. He then says a paradox that brings their obsessive legal-based intellect to a screeching halt, and as a result opened their emotions to come into play. The paradox is about the person without sin casting the first stone. Paradox is powerful in that it stops the intellect in its tracks.

"Paradox was used by Elijah in 1 Kings 18:20-40 when Elijah was up against a hostile crowd of the prophets of Baal," he continued. "Elijah mocked Baal, saying perhaps he is distracted or asleep. Paradox is used in Scripture when someone is standing up against terrible odds, and is outnumbered by a hostile adversary. St. Paul used a variation on paradox when they were about to kill him. Do you remember how he got the Pharisees and the Sadducees fighting?"

"He said he was being tried because of his belief in the future resurrection," I said.

"Exactly," David said. "Immediately the Pharisees were fighting with the Sadducees. The Romans didn't want to hear all this religious squabbling. What Paul said is like a paradoxical intervention we use in psychiatry. I love the whole use of paradox in therapy. The function of paradox is the same in psychotherapy and in the Scriptures. When one person is up against many opponents who are sure of themselves and hostile, paradox is a useful weapon. Paradox blunts the obsessive intellect and allows the opponent's emotions and concerns to emerge.

"Take Jesus and the woman whom he calls 'a dog' (Matthew 15:22-28; Mark 7:25-30)," David said, "which was a racist comment. Well, she responded to Jesus with another paradox, saying that even dogs eat the crumbs that fall from the table. Jesus loved her because she could rise to the challenge and play the game of paradox.

"What you are asking about paradox is my favorite theme in Scripture," David said. "Peter was a dullard, so Jesus named him 'the Rock.' John and James were always fighting, so Jesus named them 'the Sons of Thunder.' Jesus had a tremendous sense of humor. You want to enter the city when everyone expects you to ride in on a white charger? Try riding in on a jackass! It's hilarious."

4. Child-like Core of Our Soul

"My final question concerns the fact that every theologian I know says that humans are so created that God corresponds to our deepest longing and yearning," I said. "And every psychological theory I know says the core of our soul was laid down in our childhood. Sigmund Freud observed there was such a close correspondence between our infantile yearning and our religion that he thought religion must be a projection of what we really want and yearn for. But I think we can turn this observation around. Freud's observation proves that the theologians are right, that God has been wise in creating us such that our deepest longings and yearnings are for God. The child-like core of my soul yearns for fusion with my mother, and God is like a parent."

"That's very perceptive, profound," David said. "Unless you become like a little child you cannot enter the Kingdom of Heaven. Children are more creative and playful, and religion brings out our creativity and playfulness. Faith makes you young. It allows you to see things anew, the way a child sees things. Psalm 139 speaks of being known by God the way I felt known by the watchful eye of my mother. There is youthfulness and joyfulness in faith, as in children. This openness and playfulness comes as one yearns for God. God's huge love for us, like the love of a parent, can be understood only as we drop our adult defenses and get away from all these rules. I think this is the most profound thing you have come up with, Jeff. It really strikes mental health professionals at their roots."

Evidence of an Anti-Religion Bias in Psychiatric Research

We spoke of a subtle anti-religious bias among mental health professionals. This section reports some research data which were called to my attention by David Larson. He and his colleagues had reviewed 2,348 consecutive research papers published from 1978-82 in the four top psychiatric journals: *Archives of General Psychiatry*, the *American Journal of Psychiatry*, the *Canadian* and *British Journal of Psychiatry*. Their goal was to discover how religion was treated as a research variable.[29]

They discovered several scholarly research papers in which religious faith had emerged in the statistical data as highly significant, but where that fact was not discussed, or was dismissed in the text of the paper. In other words, the data and the text contradicted one another. Someone reading the statistical tables would arrive at the conclusion that religion was extremely helpful – often it was the most helpful variable of all. Yet if one read the text and the abstracts, and ignored the data in the tables, then one would find religion not mentioned.

They also discovered that religion is usually omitted from research on mental health. When it is studied, it is studied using primitive methods that don't do justice to religion.

Here is what David said to me, plus endnotes that will allow the reader to double check the data:

"One well-known researcher conducted a longitudinal study of alcoholism," David said. "You know the study."

"Of course," I said. "I was the U.S. Government project officer funding that research."

"George Vaillant's data showed that religion was significantly associated with abstinence from alcohol," David said, "and also Alcoholics Anonymous was significantly associated with abstinence. But then Vaillant referred to it as 'an alcohol substitute,' which is reductionistic."[30]

"I didn't know that," I said.

"In the text of his paper Vaillant implied this is simply a substitute dependency similar to valium use, marijuana use, mystical belief, prayer, meditation, compulsive work, compulsive gambling, compulsive eating, and chain smoking! As if it were going to have a harmful effect on the men, similar to the effect of alcohol. Yet that isn't what his data showed. The data showed that religion was extremely positive in its effect on alcoholism. Given there was little discussion of religion in the introduction or the discussion, the reader is unprepared for the findings in the results section.

"I'm telling you, Jeff," David continued, "you and I would get drawn and quartered if we tried to publish a research paper in which the most clinically beneficial variable in the data was not discussed in the text of the paper. Yet when the variable is religion, mental health researchers think it's OK to ignore, misinterpret, or understate it.

"There was a study of the outcome of heroin addiction," David continued. "By far the largest predictor of abstinence from heroin for a year or more is a religious program. That accounted for 43% of those abstinent. The next largest predictor is as minuscule in importance compared to religion. The variable second to religion was 19% for residence relocation."

"So how did they present their data?" I asked.

"They had to make a decision about how to write up their results for publication," David replied. "So they decided to avoid the religion variable and instead write an article on 'residence relocation.' The impact of religion was dismissed in a single sentence as being of no interest.[31] Therefore, the text of the paper says something very different than what the data in their tables showed.

"In another article about schizophrenics the largest R^2 — the largest amount of variance explained — was associated with religious activities. Yet the meaning of that observation was never discussed," David said.[32] "If you or I published a study in which we ignored a finding of that magnitude, we would be strongly reminded by the peer review process that we did not introduce the variable in the introduction, explain how we had analyzed it in the methods section, nor did we review the implications in the discussion section. However, if the ignored variable is religion, then a different standard is used. Mental health researchers try to avoid the 'R' word."

"The 'R' word?" I thought I knew what he meant.

"The 'R' word: religion," David said. "Mental health researchers treat religion with, at best, polite silence."

"I have a hard time believing that editors of a major clinical journal could publish a study in which the amount of variance explained by religion was greater than any other variable, and yet fail to speak about the issue in the text of the article," I said.

"There's another example," said David. "Greyson and Stevenson published an article on near-death experiences.[33] Now you would expect someone writing about near-death experiences to pay attention to religion. But no! Their data showed that the largest change resulting from a near-death experience was the person's attitude toward God or religion, affecting 75% of the sample. Yet this incredible fact is not mentioned in the text. It is not mentioned! There is not a single word about it in the text of the article! The tables show that 'God and religion' are twice as important in the data as 'sex, marriage.'"

"Good grief!" I was appalled. "I don't believe this can be true."

"Jerome Motto showed that absence of religion was a significant predictor of suicide," David said.[34] "Yet he never discusses religion in the text of his paper either."

"In all these articles I've been talking about," David said, "the only way you would discover that religion was important would be to read the numbers in the tables of data. Religion, which bounces out of the data as highly significant, highly correlated with the outcome variable, is ignored in the text of these papers.

"But in these studies at least a religion variable was included in the research study. The vast majority of research studies have not included any measure of religion in relationship to mental health. This is not just a deficit on the part of the authors. The editorial reviewers who read such articles do not comment, noting the absence from the text of a discussion of religious variables."

"And you read the tables of all these papers?" I puzzled. "Are you insane? How did you ever get started on such a wild goose chase?"

"When I undertook my first 'Systematic Analysis' review," he said, "we read through thousands of articles and studied their research methods, to see whether religious variables were used in the study. By that method we discovered that religion often bounces out of the data as highly significant, but it is ignored by the researchers when they write up their results. It is not mentioned."

"In the last two years women published articles demonstrating that most health-care research was about men," I said. "Women had been neglected and ignored in health research."[35]

"Yes," David said.

"Those articles had a huge impact," I continued. "Today Congress is adamant that this deficit in health research be corrected."

"Yes," David said, "I know what you are talking about."

"Well, I think you should write the corresponding article about the neglect of religion in health-care research," I said, "and publish it in the *New England Journal of Medicine.*"

"That is a really interesting idea," David said.

"You have already done the research and demonstrated that religion has a powerful positive effect not only on mental health, but on physical health also. You have demonstrated that this whole arena of research is neglected and massively under-studied throughout health-care research. No doubt this neglect has something to do with funding from the National Institutes of Health being government funding and therefore subject to the separation-of-church-and-state rule. But here we have one of the most powerful influences on health which is systematically neglected throughout health-care research. All you have to do is take your *Forgotten Factor* book and boil it down to a short *New England Journal of Medicine* article. It would be dynamite!"

"That is really an interesting idea," David said. "I think I'll do it!"

"You might be able to have an impact on the direction of research throughout the entire health-care research industry," I said. "Remember what happened when they published that article showing that women were forgotten by health-care researchers! You have the data to show that religion is a similar issue."

"Yes," David said, "that is a great idea. I think I will do it! Are you asking to be co-author on this article?"

"No," I said. "I didn't do the research. You did."

Anyone wishing to delve further into the data demonstrating that religious faith is healthy in the physical and mental health research literature should obtain the book by David and Susan Larson, *The Forgotten Factor in Physical and Mental Health: What Does the Research Show?*

Then saith he unto them, My **soul** is exceeding sorrowful, even unto death: tarry ye here, and watch with me.
(KJV: Matthew 26:38)

Then he said to them, "I am deeply grieved, even unto death; remain here, and stay awake with me."
(NRSV: Matthew 26:38)

Comparing the King James Version of 1611 to the New Revised Standard Version of 1989:

Moreover I call God for a record upon my **soul**, that to spare you I came not as yet unto Corinth.

(KJV: 2 Corinthians 1:23)

But I call on God as witness against **me**: it was to spare you that I did not come again to Corinth.

(NRSV: 2 Corinthians 1:23)

Chapter 10
Comment by Krister Stendahl

"Soul is a beautiful word," Stendahl reflected. "One of the reasons I came to like this word 'soul' is that it has something to do with God. 'Soul' suggests a Godwardness.

"In the New Testament there was such an eschatological sense," Stendahl continued, "such an impending sense of the Apocalypse. Everything was viewed in that perspective. Thus the emphasis is on how God will judge the soul; it is a soul under judgment. This is quite different from what I find in Genesis 2:7. There we find a functional soul, a being in relationship to other beings."

His comment led me to think that the mental health view of the soul is closer to the Old Testament than to the New. A person is seen in relationship with other people within mental health theory: a soul relating to other souls, a being relating to other beings. That is the "functional soul" of the Old Testament.

The New Testament concept that the soul has a future beyond death, and that we are invited today to begin living by the values of the Kingdom, is an aspect of human life usually ignored in psychotherapy. The New Testament view of a soul under judgment is often considered guilt-inducing when non-Christian psychotherapists are honest about what they really feel.

"In Genesis 2:7 there are two elements that are brought together: God's breath and the dust," Stendahl continued. "Humans by nature are human and divine. But the point of Genesis 2:7 is that it all hangs together. The emphasis is on the unity, not on the duality. That is why *nephesh* is translated 'being' in Genesis 2:7 in modern Bibles. What word could better express the idea of a unity than the word 'being?'"

Historically, there had been a debate about Genesis 2:7. In the *King James Version* it says:

> And the LORD God formed man of the dust of the ground, and breathed into his nostrils the breath of life; and man became a living soul. (KJV: Genesis 2:7)

But in most modern translations the last phrase in the sentence is translated 'living being.' The Church Fathers and about eighteen centuries of Christian tradition thought this verse referred to two aspects of human nature: body and soul, a duality. But during the Twentieth Century, biblical scholars have emphasized the unity of the personality as seen in the older books of the Hebrew Old Testament.

Dr. David Larson

"In this chapter we just read about David Larson," Stendahl continued, "you quote him as saying, 'God loves me. That is what I keep finding. There is hardly anything negative. I would have expected more criticism. But there isn't. It is almost entirely positive, like a huge pillow of love.'

"I think perhaps Larson is a little too self-congratulatory," he said. "Perhaps a little more fear and trembling before the Lord might be called for."

"This guy Larson has been more courageous than any other psychiatrist," I said. "He has spoken up as a researcher, shown that religious variables are missing from health research. When they are present in the data, they are

ignored and discriminated against when the researchers write up their results. I don't think he should be criticized."
"So he has been courageous?" Stendahl said. "Putting his career at risk for the sake of his faith?"
"Yes," I replied.
"Even so," he said, "I don't think a person can ever rest with complete assurance."
"You want to avoid the idea of cheap grace," I said.
"Yes," he replied.
As he said this I could feel my stomach tie up in a knot. Neither I nor Stendahl nor anyone else could simply rest assured that God supported our efforts. I felt fear and trembling in my bones. His comments reminded me of something Jesus said:

> Who among you would say to your slave who has just come in from plowing or tending the field, "Come here at once and take your place at the table?" Would you not rather say to him, "Prepare supper for me, put on your apron and serve me while I eat and drink; later you may eat and drink"? Do you thank the slave for doing what was commanded? So you also, when you have done all that you were ordered to do, say, "We are worthless slaves; we have done only what we ought to have done!" (NRSV: Luke 17:7-10).

As a worthless slave seeking to serve God, I have written this book.

The comforter that should relieve my **soul** is far from me.

(KJV: Lamentations 1:16)

For a comforter is far from me, one to revive my **courage**.

(NRSV: Lamentations 1:16)

Chapter 11
John Young, M.D.

John Young is a psychiatrist and Catholic priest in the Order of Holy Cross. He was on the faculty at Yale Medical School for many years. Actually, he trained at Yale in the year after me, which is how we met. In the last few years John felt called to work in Whiting Forensic Hospital, a hospital for the criminally insane in Connecticut. Like other psychiatrist-priests, John is attracted toward working with the indigent and chronically mentally ill. John remains active in his order, celebrates Mass regularly. He keeps his vows: poverty, celibacy, obedience. He still lives in New Haven.

1. Psychiatrists Treat the Soul
I presented to John the idea that there is a biblical soul which includes all of the *psyche* of psychiatry, but which also includes our relatedness to God.[36]

"That makes a lot of sense to me," John said. "From reading the Psalms during Bible study, I have noticed that the word 'soul' is much richer than the way we use the word today. It means the whole person."

"Exactly," I said. "The biblical soul was the whole person, or at least the whole personality. I have written a book focused on the idea that 'Your soul is who you are.'"[37]

"I've always been unhappy with the anti-religious stance that is attributed to psychiatry," he said. "Freud was an extreme example. I don't experience any incompatibility of religion and psychiatry. I think there is a religious dimension of hospitalized psychiatry."

"Do you think that which you treat as a psychiatrist is the biblical soul?" I asked.

"Yes," he said, "I think that is what I do. After being a psychiatrist all these years, I finally figured out that there are two principles that summarize all my work in psychiatry and in the priesthood. The first big issue is to help people learn how they come across to other people. Usually a patient in my hospital will discover that other people see him as being more impaired than he realized. The second big issue is that I want to get people to treat each other right. Expert witnesses in court should treat people right, patients should treat people right. What it comes down to is having the proper respect for the other person as a soul. People should treat each other right whether they are religious or not. It is because there is more to a person than just the *psyche*. Because the person is a soul, even if he has killed someone, he is valuable."

"You mentioned two big issues that pervade your work," I said. "How does the first of these relate to the biblical soul? What is the relationship of soul to the idea of teaching people how they are perceived by other people?"

"I don't know," he said. "I just know that it is very important. I run a group on Friday afternoons. Me and the patients at my hospital sit around. I bring food. And they discuss how they see one another. It is often the first time they have come to understand how they come across to other people. It is very important. Can you tell me how that relates to the idea of soul?"

"One of my ideas about the soul is that my soul is who I truly am in the eyes of God," I said. "It is based on the assumption that God knows me even better than my psychoanalyst knows me."

"That's hard to argue with," John said. "It sounds like a good definition."

"So the important part of my soul is not who I think I am," I said, "but how God perceives me."

"Yes," John said, sounding interested.

"And how God sees me," I said, groping through new ideas, "is probably closer to how other people see me than it is to how I see myself."

"That's great," John said. "Other patients see who a guy really is. The way other patients see a man is close to who he really is. And the truth is how God sees him."

"You got it," I said.

2. God's View of Our Soul

"Another question, John," I said. "If God has a view of who John Young is, can you somehow come to know what that view is?"

"Oh yes," he replied. "Spirituality is always based on some variation of that. The aesthetical writers spoke of it. There was a popular paperback a few years ago, *The Cloud of Unknowing*, about that subject.[38] This aesthetic ideal means contemplating or praying at a high level. It is a wordless form of prayer. One subsists, remaining open to the presence of God. God's will as it applies to that person is absorbed."

"What about your personal experience?" I had grown restless with his abstract generalizations. "Do you have direct experience of this?"

"A couple of times every day," he said, "for a few moments. I cannot say it is a sustained experience. It's an ideal. This is an authentic and valid description of what the saints were about. The tradition talks about a purgative way of prayer, which is not what you are talking about. Then there is a unitive way of prayer, which is what you are talking about. It means becoming one with God, insofar as we can. Becoming one with what God intends. To come to know God's will. Which usually means expressing God's love and avoiding evil."

Six months later, I asked John if he had given any more thought to finding out how God perceives him.

"It's been on my mind constantly since you mentioned it," John said. "I've not been thinking about it. It is not the kind of thing one thinks about. I've been praying that there will be a convergence of my view of myself and God's view of me.

I would like my self-concept to be isomorphic with God's view. It's more of a communion through prayer than a thinking process."

"One person I interviewed said that the discrepancy between our self-concept and God's concept," I said, "is a measure of mental illness. Does that make sense to you? She said that usually people underestimate themselves compared with the potential that God sees."

"Yes, that makes a lot of sense," John said. "Who said that?"

"A Jewish social worker," I replied.

"I like that idea," John said. "It's fundamentally profound. It would go along with the idea that we all have a bit of mental illness or craziness in us. Of course, it would also go along with the idea of my patient who says that all mental illness is spiritual illness, and therefore he should be let out of the prison hospital."

3. A Paradox About the Soul

"A different question," I said. "Jesus said that whoever seeks his life will lose it and who loses his life for Jesus' sake will find it. The word *psyche*, which is translated 'life,' could also be translated 'self' or 'soul.' Does that paradox make sense to you?"

"The Lexionary translation of that passage is 'self,'" John said. "'He who seeks his self will lose it and who loses his self for Christ will find it.' And yes, of course it makes sense. No question about it."

"What does it mean?" I asked.

"If you try to take care of Number One as your exclusive focus," he said, "you will lose what you are seeking. But if you set that aside and lose it in some fundamental sense, because you are following Jesus, you will find both that which you were looking for and a lot more besides."

"But doesn't that teaching run contrary to an important current in mental health theory?" I asked.

"You mean vital pursuit of the self?" John asked. "Accepting oneself, getting in touch with yourself? No. I'm not sure that contradicts what Jesus said. You must be referring to the teachings of Heinz Kohut about Self Psychology?"

"No," I said, "I was referring to a lot of therapists out there who are teaching that self-actualization or self-realization or individuation or self-fulfillment, or fulfilling your potential, is the ultimate goal of life. I've heard hundreds of psychotherapists say to clients, 'You've got to learn to take better care of yourself.'"

"Well," John said, "there are always stupid followers. But I'm not sure Heinz Kohut ever said anything like that. I don't think there is an opposition of Kohut and Jesus."

"It seems to me that the goal of psychoanalytic therapy can be stated in negative or positive terms," I said. "In negative terms it's easier to swallow. The goal of therapy is to get away from the false self, the lies and rationalization and denial caused by narcissism. I think Christianity and Self Psychology would converge vis-a-vis that goal. The problem would be when the goal is stated positively. If a therapist teaches that the goal of therapy is to seek the self, then Jesus' paradox would contradict that."

"Yeah," John said, "but I don't think Kohut ever said it in a positive way like that."

"Of course not," I said, "because Kohut's whole therapeutic effort was directed at narcissistic personality disorder. The last thing you would tell someone narcissistic is that they should go and seek their self.

"Professor Krister Stendahl is a New Testament scholar," I continued, "who says that one would not want to talk about loss of the self as a way of finding the soul, if you were addressing a person who is depressed. Nor would you want to say that to someone who has a shattered 'self' because of early life abuse, child abuse. To such an audience one might better speak of 'justification by faith alone.' What do you think of this comment?"

"Well," John said, "he has a point. Whenever one is trying to give a message, one should think carefully about the addressee and where they are coming from. If you tell someone who is depressed and suicidal that they should pray more and read the Bible more, you are not going to help them much. That's what is written in the textbooks on pastoral counseling. I agree with the tenor of what Krister Stendahl says.

"Hopefully through helping the person," he continued, "they could respond enough so they would reach the point where they could hear the next thing. There are different stages of faith. It's like you can't learn differential equations until you learn algebra, and you can't learn algebra until you learn to add and subtract. The person who doesn't have a 'self' is like someone struggling to learn arithmetic. Perhaps through the deprivations of early childhood a 'self' never formed, or it was severely damaged. The first step is to build up a 'self.' You can't tell someone to give up something they don't have. The person who has no 'self,' or whose 'self' is shattered, cannot give up their 'self' for Christ until they have a 'self' in the first place. Once they have a 'self,' then you might be able to suggest they give it up, but that is like differential equations."

4. Child-like Core of Our Soul

"Another idea I have," I said, "is that Freud said religion taps into childish regression. Yet child-like regression is the source of our playfulness, creativity, renewal, rebirth, and enjoyment of folderol. It seems to me that Freud's observation, rather than negating religion, proves that the theologians were right when they said that our soul is so created that God corresponds to our deepest yearnings. What do you think of that idea?"

"I think you're right," John said, "but it isn't so clear where Freud stood on religion. His thirty years of correspondence with Pastor Oskar Pfister is powerful evidence that he wasn't so one-sided as he appeared to be in *Future of an Illusion*."

"Did I tell you that a friend and I are finally translating Pfister's essay into English?" I asked.

"Yes," John said, "I think it is time that someone translated Pfister's rebuttal to Freud. What was it called?"

"*Illusion of a Future*," I said. This essay is an appendix of this book. Pfister is also discussed in Chapter 17.

Chapter 12
Louisa Mattson, Ph.D.

Dr. Louisa Mattson is a clinical psychologist in Acton, Massachusetts.[39] She works closely with the clergy in that area. She speaks of "psychotherapy as a spiritual adventure."

1. Psychologists Treat the Soul

I asked Dr. Mattson if the "self" treated by psychologists is the "soul," or some aspect of the "soul."

"When I'm doing good therapy," she replied, "I'm doing soulful things. I would think soulful things are different than spiritual things."

"What is the difference?" I asked.

"'Soulful' would include a certain organic basis which I think is missing from 'spiritual,'" she replied. "Thus the spirit is clearly different from the body, but the soul includes both, I think. By the way, do you know the recent book by Thomas Moore about the soul?"[40]

"Yes," I said, "of course. It's an interesting book!"

"He's coming at it more from a Jungian perspective," she said.

"I think Carl Jung had a different meaning of the word 'soul' than the Bible," I replied. "In Jung the soul is neither the whole person nor the whole personality. Jung's use of the term 'soul' is closer to Plato's use of the word than it is to the biblical term."***

"I don't know enough about the Bible to really answer your question," she said, "but I do think the Jungian 'soul' is different than the biblical 'soul.'"

"In many places in the Bible the word 'soul' may have referred to either the whole person or the whole personality," I replied. "Of course, it is difficult to know exactly what the Bible said. Two weeks ago I went to the Society of Biblical Literature convention in San Francisco. I asked forty-three biblical scholars whether they think psychiatrists and psychologists today treat what in biblical times would have been called the 'soul.' A majority of them said 'yes.' But it is a complex issue."[41]

2. God's View of Our Soul

"Do you think that God's view of Louisa Mattson can be known?" I asked.

"I think I can get glimmers of it," she said, "but I don't think I can know fully who God thinks I am. I get glimmers of it through visceral experience rather than through cognition. It's a sense of being on the right track, of tapping into something. For example, when a client has made a turnaround in therapy, my tiny office feels like it opens up,

---

*** Carl Jung wrote of a "soul," which he called the *anima* or *animus*. This "soul" was not the whole person, nor the whole personality. The "soul" of Jung was in touch with "Archetypes" in a place he called the "Collective Unconscious."

Plato wrote of a "soul" which was less than the whole person, and which was in touch with the Forms in the Realm of Pure Being. Thus there appear to be close parallels between Carl Jung's concept of the "soul" and Plato's concept. In both cases we could say, "You *have* a soul."

In contrast to those ideas, the "soul" of the Bible was not so mysterious. It was what we would call the "personality" or the "whole person" today. Thus when one says "Jesus saves one's soul," it means, "Jesus saves one's self." It means one will be transformed as a whole person in a New Creation.

Biblical scholars often say, "You don't *have* a soul, you *are* a soul!" Thus the Bible contrasts with both Plato and Carl Jung.

as if the whole universe has somehow come into my office, which is actually quite small. God says I'm on the right track. 'Love' is the key to the whole thing."

3. A Paradox About the Soul

"Jesus said that anyone who seeks to save their life will lose it," I said, "but anyone who loses it for Jesus will find it. The Greek word *psyche*, which is translated 'life,' could also be translated 'self.' Does it make sense to you to say that anyone who seeks their self will lose it, and anyone who loses it for Jesus will save it?"

"Absolutely," she replied. "I distinguish the small 'self' from the larger 'Self.' To seek the small 'self' is to pursue security needs and ego needs. But if you let go of that, then larger life enters in and you discover you're larger than your skin-encapsulated 'self.' It's like my experience as a new mother. I constantly have to play catch-up with who my sons are. I may think I know who they are, but I discover they've changed and are no longer that person. I have to mourn the loss of the baby and be open to who they are now."

"And who they are now is the larger 'Self'?" I asked.

"Yes, there is a fluidity to who they are," she said. "My sons are connecting to something larger than who I thought they were yesterday. That is the way I think of 'spirituality.' 'Spirituality' is the art of making connections. I got that idea from Alan Jones' book *Soul Making*.[42] The idea of making connections between the soul and something larger is also found in the books that are coming out now on 'deep ecology.' The deep ecologists talk about expanding the 'Self' to include the whole world. There's a book I like called *Thinking Like a Mountain*."[43]

"Going back to the issue of losing the 'self' in order to find it," I said, "there is a New Testament professor named Krister Stendahl who suggests that this is a reasonable teaching for someone who has a sense of 'self,' but is not a reasonable thing to tell someone whose 'self' has been shattered or is non-existent, perhaps because of childhood incest or some other disasters. What do you think of that idea?"

"Yes," she replied. "I agree because I am a westerner. In the West we find that you first have to have a self in order to move beyond it. But in Asia I don't think that is true. I think the Buddhists would say it is crazy to say that you must have a self. I'm into Buddhist meditation."

"As a therapist," I asked, "do you sometimes tell clients they must focus more on their own needs, and pay more attention to who they are?"

"Absolutely," she replied. "As a therapist I almost always tell clients they need to think about their own needs, and pay more attention to their own 'self.'"

4. Child-like Core of Our Soul

"Another question," I said. "It seems to me that Sigmund Freud indicted religion as being a projection of what people really want on a child-like level. We all want to be known and protected, for example. It seems to me that Freud was simply expressing what Christian theologians have always said, which is that God has so created us that our deepest yearnings are for God. If our deepest yearnings are our most child-like yearnings, then God fulfills them. This is not an indictment of the religion; rather it is one of the strengths of the religion. What do you think of that idea?"

"Definitely," she replied. "I've lived long enough so that all the authority figures I looked up to have failed me, failed to live up to my perfectionistic expectations. I still hold onto the hope that God won't fail me, that God will ultimately come through as worthy of my trust, will protect me, and that God knows everything there is to know. You see, I am still looking for the perfect parent. I like it better when you call this yearning 'child-like' rather than 'childish.'"

"'Childish' is pejorative," I said. "'Child-like' is not."

"Yes," she said. "Christianity leaves you feeling totally loved and protected, but at the same time it stretches you beyond your limits. It stretches you beyond what you know. It is a paradox. At the same time that Christianity meets your needs for security, it asks you to give up your needs for security, to relinquish all those things that you cling to in order to make yourself feel safe."

Chapter 13
Larry Schulte, Ph.D.

Dr. Larry Schulte is a clinical psychologist on the faculty of the California School of Professional Psychology in Alhambra, a suburb of Los Angeles. Larry is a Catholic layman. He almost became a monk before getting trained as a psychologist. Now he is happily married. He also works with the archdiocese on a program for bereavement in Catholic churches in California. Larry's enthusiasm for this book is a large part of what carried me through some despondent times when I thought it might prove a waste of time. The reason I thought that is because no one agreed with me, no one except Larry.

1. Psychologists Treat the Soul

"Your statement that the *psyche* which we treat in psychology is an aspect of the biblical soul makes a lot of sense to me, Jeff," he said.[44] "It reminds me of a patient I treated in private practice. Her soul had been extinguished, or never discovered. She came to me with panic disorder. I treated her with existential psychotherapy. During the therapy a history of incest emerged. That was how her soul got extinguished. The therapy turned out to be a rediscovery of her soul. She said that I was her healer and not just her therapist."

I was reminded of Alan Broadhead's comments about "soul murder" in Chapter 1.

"What do you mean that her soul had been extinguished?" I puzzled.

"She had lost a sense of meaning across her life," Larry said. "She was going through the motions of life, but it had no meaning. She felt empty. She had nothing superior giving her a sense of core meaning. By working through the incest she began to blossom. It all started one day when she said, 'I need to know more about your spiritual beliefs.' Without compromising boundaries, I told her I was a Christian and a believer. Had I not told her that, the therapy would have remained limited to the cognitive and behavioral aspects of panic disorder. It would not have been as healing. She began to free-associate about a spiritual cleanliness inside. She wrote me a poem. During the termination phase, she talked about there being new life inside her. Not resurrection. New life."

It sounded to me like a highly positive transference.

"Let's go back to the basic question," I said. "How would you define the 'soul?'"

"It is the spirit of life which gives people resilience," he said. "It gives them the ability to go on and on and on, like the Israelis trudging forty years in the desert. They had resilience."

2. God's View of Our Soul

"Another question," I said. "If God has a view of who Larry Schulte is, can you know or discern some aspects of that? You know what I say, that God knows me even better than my psychoanalyst."

"Yeah," Larry said, laughing. "Very definitely I can know how God sees me. This is a hard one, this question. I know it through the creative process. That doesn't necessarily mean music. By being a co-creator with God. That is how I know how God sees me. I am at that moment part of God. The creative process is best represented by agape love. It is also evident in the conception of children through sexual intercourse. I also experience it in art forms. The opposite of that would be anything that would extinguish agape love, such as selfishness."

3. A Paradox About the Soul

I presented my favorite paradox and asked if it made any sense to him. The paradox is that whoever would find his soul will lose, and whoever loses his soul (or self) for Christ will find it.

"I would say that is the definition of agape love," Larry said.

"What?" I said.

"By losing yourself through meeting the needs of others," he explained. "Agape love means selfless going out to meet the needs of others. If you don't do that you lose your self. It involves being in a community. If you don't do it, you remain lost."

"Does this idea contradict certain trends in psychotherapy?" I asked.

"I don't think so," he said. "What were you thinking of?"

"People sometimes say the goal of therapy is self-actualization or fulfilling your potential, and so on," I explained.

"There's no contradiction," Larry said. "These teachings go hand in hand. True self-actualization is for other people. As I understand Abraham Maslow's hierarchy of needs,[45] once you have met your basic needs, there is the need for altruism, for giving to the other. In Irving Yallom's latest book, *Love's Executioner*, he talks about what makes therapy is a relationship of sharing."[46]

"My New Testament teacher, Krister Stendahl, suggests that self-denial is not something one should discuss indiscriminately," I said. "He says that we should be careful not to advocate loss of the soul or self to a patient who is depressed. Nor would one talk about that to someone whose self had been shattered in infancy by neglect or child abuse. One might rather talk about God's grace to that audience. What do you think of this?"

"Absolutely," Larry said. "I agree. They don't have the ego strength to understand and go with it. If someone were paranoid or self-deprecating, then talking to them about selfless love might convince them that they are not capable of selfless love, and therefore worsen the depression. The idea of selflessly giving of your 'self' for other people — agape love — can be understood only by someone with enough ego strength."

4. Child-like Core of Our Soul

I presented my ideas about how religion relates to and validates the child-like core of my soul.

"Yeah," Larry said. "You're talking about God as a good daddy or mommy. It's what keeps the fearless sense of self alive. Like yesterday I was at a party in Hollywood Hills. We were on the deck of a house perched over a cliff. The house was on stilts. It was a 500-foot drop off the back of the deck. And this child that came with my friends was playing on the deck without any sense of fear at all. The child was not terrified that there was a 500-foot drop. That fearless playfulness is called faith. It's what Franciscan theology is built on, you know."

"Wait!" I said. "I don't know. Explain."

"Franciscan theology, especially the early descriptions of Saint Francis, is full of a jovial spirit even in the face of hardship," Larry said. "Even when carrying the cross there can be true joy because there is perfect love.

"And Liberation Theology is similar," he continued, "when it talks about social injustice. What keeps people going is not the sense of righting a wrong, because often the injustices can't be corrected. The motivating force is love for other people. One recognizes that one can't make a huge difference, but you can make a small difference. And that difference is selfless love.

"When I see all the pain of people in my psychotherapy office," Larry said, "it is obvious that something religious is needed and not just therapy. People need a sense of other, and selfless giving. Like this woman who is director of the adolescent church school program at my church. She has suffered so much abuse and pain in her life and it is not possible for her to simply confront her pain and untangle it.

The only way she can live is by giving something of herself to others. When she gives of herself to adolescents, their comments make it obvious to her that she is valuable and needed. That contradicts all those old tapes inside her head from her childhood, which tell her she is worthless. Her work is far more valuable than an anti-depressant medicine. I say this without meaning to slight psychopharmacology. This woman says she is rising above all her psychological problems and finding meaning through giving her self in relationships with others."

"I always love talking with you, Larry," I said.

"You know I love talking with you," he said. "Please mail me your manuscript. Soon. I really want to read it."

All the **souls** that came with Jacob into Egypt, which came out of his loins, besides Jacob's sons' wives, all the **souls** were threescore and six; And the sons of Joseph, which were born him in Egypt, were two **souls**: all the **souls** of the house of Jacob, which came into Egypt, were threescore and ten.

(KJV: Genesis 46:26-27)

All the **persons** belonging to Jacob who came into Egypt, who were his own offspring, not including the wives of his sons, were sixty-six **persons** in all. The children of Joseph, who were born to him in Egypt, were two; all the **persons** of the house of Jacob who came into Egypt were seventy.

(NRSV: Genesis 46:26-27)

Chapter 14
Comment by Krister Stendahl

"There is such a strong theocentric view throughout your book," Professor Krister Stendahl said. "You stress that to view a soul you must understand the relationship with God. But you neglect something. Christ gave us two commandments. You say that Christ taught us to love God with all one's heart and all one's soul. What you neglect is that there is a second commandment: 'You should love your neighbor as yourself.'

"In the next chapter, you say a child relates to its mother in a symbiosis that continues in the relationship with God," Stendahl continued. "But that symbiosis also continues in our interdependence — we are part of the human family. So there is a triangular relationship of me, God, and my neighbor. This kind of relationship with another person is illustrated, I think, by sexual intercourse. This is the most intense analogy to what you mean when you say that to lose yourself is to gain yourself. It is about giving and receiving. It's about a symbiosis with another person. This also happens to be the moment when new life is conceived."

"You are right," I said. "But there is a reason that I have gone overboard stressing the relationship between the soul and God. It is because that aspect is ignored in most psychotherapy. The relationship between the soul and neighbor is not ignored. The relationship between a husband and wife is not ignored. But the vertical dimension is usually missing. This is why my book overemphasizes the first commandment at the expense of the second."

Translation of *Psyche*

"Let me ask you again," I said. "There are many biblical scholars who think that I have mistranslated the biblical saying about how loss of soul leads to finding the soul (Matthew 16:25; Mark 8:35; Luke 9:24; 17:33; John 12:25). They say that *psyche* in that verse can be translated only as 'life'."

"I think you should leave it," Stendahl said. "To translate *psyche* as 'life' makes it sound as if Christ were speaking only of martyrdom. It ignores the interpretation of self-denial and a sacrificial lifestyle."

The Next Chapter

"In the next chapter," Stendahl said, "you really begin to speak for yourself. You write with such joy! That is really a powerful chapter. When was it you thought you heard God calling you to write this book, during prayers? What was the year?"

"It was when I was a minister in Beverly Farms and Manchester," I replied, "on the North Shore of Boston. It was the year after I graduated from the Divinity School — about a quarter of a century ago."

"So the timing is what you say in your book? It was before you ever thought of getting trained in the mental health field."

"That's right," I said. "Up until then it had never crossed my mind to go to medical school. I had never thought of getting trained in the mental health field. It was because of that sense of being called that I went to medical school and became a psychiatrist."

For thou hast considered my trouble; thou hast known my **soul** in adversities.

(KJV: Psalm 31:7)

You have seen my affliction; you have taken heed of my adversities.

(NRSV: Psalm 31:7)

I said, Lord, be merciful unto me: heal my **soul**;
for I have sinned against thee.

(KJV: Psalm 41:4)

As for me, I said, "O Lord, be gracious to me;
heal **me**, for I have sinned against you."

(NRSV: Psalm 41:4)

Your Soul Is
Who You Really Are

Though I were perfect, yet would I not know my **soul.**

(KJV: Job 9:21)

I am blameless; I do not know my**self.**

(NRSV: Job 9:21)

Chapter 15
What Is a Human Being?

Is there more to being human than the mental health movement knows?

Most mental health clinicians would say that they deal with all a client's thoughts, feelings, and relationships. But religion is avoided in most psychotherapy. "Religiosity" is interpreted psychologically.

Knowing this, most patients with faith, in my experience, avoid discussing religion with their psychotherapists.

More often than not, faith is treated as if it were on one planet, and the mental health movement on another.

Where does the psychological part of me end and the religious part begin? How do we construct a Berlin Wall so as to subdivide "me" into the secular and the sacred part?

Some people speak of their identity as if it were subdivided along the same lines as our society. When people use the Platonic phrase "body, mind, and spirit," they reflect the way our society works. Primary care physicians are different than mental health specialists, who are different than the clergy. Thus the fragmented way our society deals with a human being is reflected in a fragmented sense of our own identity.

I take a different approach. My identity is undivided. My self-concept cannot be split.

My identity is who I am in relationship with God, and with my neighbor. As such my identity has both a physical and an emotional component. Thus my "soul" or identity is expressed through my physical life, my emotional life, and my prayer life. Who I am, i.e. my "soul," is expressed through exercise, relationships, emotions, thoughts, and faith.

Three aspects of my "self" are ignored by the mental health movement:

A. The relationship between God and me;
B. My future after death;
C. The invitation to begin today living by the values of the Kingdom of God.

In these three respects I am not fully known by any therapist I have ever seen. In other words, the mental health movement deals with who I am (i.e. my "soul"), but not all of who I am.

My Odyssey

It will help if I explain how I came to think as I do. It is the saga of how a minister became a psychiatrist, and how I stumbled on my soul.

Twenty-five years ago I was a fulltime minister in St. John's Episcopal Church in Beverly Farms and Manchester by the Sea, north of Boston. I obtained an unusual answer to my prayers. I had asked God to use me for whatever purpose God wanted. During those prayers I conceived the wild notion of writing a book about the soul. It looked impossible. Yet it was a fascinating idea. No one was talking about the "soul" in my experience. It appeared to me that the mental health movement was treating what I thought was the "soul."

This amusing idea of writing a book about the soul, which percolated through my brain during prayers, can claim only my own brain for its authority. I have no way of knowing whether God put the idea in my brain. All I know is that the thought first arose when I was praying for God to use me for whatever purpose God wanted.

What troubled me then was the juxtaposition of the New Testament Greek word *psyche* and its English translation, "soul." In contemporary America the *psyche* was the focus of *psychi*atry and *psychol*ogy, but was presumed to have nothing to do with the soul. Therefore, I was unable to imagine writing this book. I had no credentials. I informed God that the idea was impossible, and that God should forget it because I wasn't going to do it. However, as I continued to pray, I continued to have this idea lodged in my brain. Eventually I caved in.

To prepare myself for this project, I decided to get trained in mental health. First, I went to the Carl Jung Institute in Zürich, Switzerland. Then I decided it would be better if I became a psychiatrist. I went four years through Case Western Reserve Medical School, obtaining an M.D. For another four years, I trained in a psychiatry residency at Yale Medical School. For seven years, I was on the faculty of the National Institute of Mental Health. I helped to write the diagnostic manual in psychiatry, *DSM-3R*.[47] Some of my work was published in the *New England Journal of Medicine,* and in the leading psychiatric journals.[48] I contributed to the leading textbooks in psychiatry. Then I went back and joined the Yale Medical School faculty, in the Department of Psychiatry, for a number of years. Today I am chairman of psychiatry at an urban teaching hospital.

From time to time I run worship services, preach, and serve communion, filling in for another minister.

During the years of preparing myself for this insane task, I forgot the original assignment. I got distracted by how attractive it was to be successful as a psychiatrist. I didn't want to jeopardize my career by publishing a book in an area that might offend the promotions committee at an academic department of psychiatry. In the interests of personal success, I forgot about this embarrassing "soul."

During those years of professional success, if someone had asked me, "What about your idea?" I would have replied, "What idea?"

"To write a book about the soul."

"That is a preposterous idea," I would have replied.
In midlife I was lost in a thicket, finding my life futile,
sterile, and without direction. I felt like Dante:

> Upon the journey of our life midway
> I came upon myself in a dark wood,
> For from the straight path I had gone astray.
> Ah, how hard is the telling what a drear
> And savage and entangled wood it was . . . .[49]

Trying to understand who I was, seeking a path through
the entangled wood, I entered Freudian psychoanalysis. I
peered into the darkness within me. Meditating, I found I was
nobody. I felt bewildered and lost. Then slowly I discerned in
that interior vacuum a faint light. It was a fantasy. Studying
the light closely, I found it amusing, but knew not the
meaning. The light grew brighter in my imagination. It
seemed to blink rapidly, as if transmitting a message at a high
baud rate. Then I saw it was my old assignment, the "Mission:
Impossible," to write a book on the soul.

"I am going nuts," I told my analyst. "This is absurd, an
inner light, a wild idea from my prayer life decades ago!" He
being a Freudian from Vienna, I was confident he would
concur.

Instead, he challenged me to take my religion more
seriously. "You have two professional identities, not just one,"
he said. "Many of your problems may not be neurotic in
origin. Some of what may be upsetting you is that you have
a religious calling that is shaking you to your bones."

"I want to disown this idea of writing a book!" I declared.

"Perhaps you are disowning what you really want," my
analyst replied. "Perhaps you should consider writing a book."

"God chooses the most unexpected messengers," I thought.
Years later, I learned my Freudian analyst was a Lutheran.

Without my being aware of it, I had been working on this
problem of the "soul" in my unconscious for decades. My
ideas about the soul are idiosyncratic, sort of a home brew I
concocted during twenty-five years of pondering the problem.

It dawned on me that, like the man who re-invented the wheel, I must not be the only person who ever thought of the soul. I set out to find other people to interview who had a joint interest in mental health and religion.

After twenty-five years of working on this problem, I now have the credentials and self-confidence to say what I originally suspected. My *psyche* or "self" is but the earthly aspect of my "soul." Mental health clinicians treat all a person's thoughts and feelings, all a person's relationships, with one exception. Thus, with one key exception, the mental health movement knows what it means to be human.

The exception is that a person's thoughts, feelings, and relationship with God are usually excluded from view in the mental health arena. If not excluded, it is interpreted psychologically, which still misses the point. Thus there is more to the "soul" than is visible in the mental health "self." What is missing from the mental health view is the core, the hub, the center of the soul.

How to Conceptualize This Soul

If the soul is known to the mental health movement, but not all the soul, then we have opened Pandora's Box. How are we to understand this soul?

My idea of the soul makes it elusive and intangible. I think your soul is who you are. The opposite is also true: who you are is your soul.

The mental health movement deals only with that which a therapist can see of a person's identity. The soul, however, is God's view of a person's identity. Therapists may approximate how God would view a client. But there is much of the client's identity which is never visible to a therapist, because religious patients tend to avoid talking to therapists about their faith, wanting not to cast the pearls of faith before someone whom they suspect might be a pig (Matthew 7:6).

Prayer is like psychotherapy. Doubters should try reading Augustine's *Confessions*. The entire book is a confessional prayer with the psychological impact of good psychother-apy.[50]

The other way I know who I am and who I am meant to be is through relationships with others in the church.

Self-Denial

Faith does not encourage self-seeking. Even soul-seeking is alien to faith.

Faith is not a quest for my identity. It is a quest for God. Faith means living as if God could be trusted. Faith also means living as if my neighbor is as important as I am, even if my neighbor is hostile and torments me.

We discover, therefore, a paradox. Jesus said it often, that whoever seeks the *psyche* will lose it but who loses it for Christ's sake will find it.

In the interviews in the preceding chapters, we learned that the goal of longterm psychotherapy is sometimes stated as being self-actualization, self-realization, individuation, self-fulfillment, or fulfilling one's potential. There are two different ways of understanding what this means. One way encourages self-seeking, the other self-forgetting. Only the second approach is consistent with my paradoxical idea about the soul.

In other words, the two top priorities in life can be stated this way:

1. You shall love "X" with all your heart, and with all your soul, and with all your strength;

2. You shall love your neighbor as yourself.

According to one interpretation of self-actualization the word "X" would be "your True Self." According to the Christian interpretation "X" would be "God." "Your True Self" would not even make the priority list.

Both Christianity and most mental health theorists would agree on the second of these two commandments. The first commandment, however, is controversial in the mental health field.

My identity is never known to me, except in retrospect. I discover who I am as I seek God in the adventure called life. Living in utter confusion about who I am, I suddenly turn a corner in the path, and discover a mirror which reflects me candidly. When this revelation comes, usually I see a more positive image of myself in God's mirror than my own self-appraisal.

For example, during the years when I was striving to build a successful academic career in psychiatry, I was terrified to write about the soul. I was afraid the promotions committee at a medical school would think poorly of any psychiatrist who wrote about religion (see David Larson's comments in Chapter 9). I hid my lantern beneath a bushel basket for fear of being discriminated against (Matthew 5:14-16). On the other hand, who I really am would become evident as I wrote a book called *Soul Psychology*.[51]

The Child-Like Core of My Soul

Like every other psychology, our Soul Psychology must start with an understanding of human development. My identity today is established upon the foundation laid in my childhood.

The core of my soul, which is the core of my personality, was established during the first eighteen months of life, I think, before I had any language. Therefore, there is something pre-linguistic and mystical about the core of me.

Every theologian I know says that our religion brings our conscious mind into alignment with the core of our soul. So the question arises, what was I like during the first eighteen months? What are the qualities, the attitudes, and the assumptions of the core of my soul?

Margaret Mahler's book, *The Psychological Birth of the Human Infant*, is the classic source of information about the psychology of infants.[52] So are Dr. Donald Winnicott's works.[53]

Based on this, and my psychoanalysis and reading in the psychiatric field, I have come to believe that there are eight characteristics of the infantile core of my soul. These are characteristics which reflect the mindset of infants, and which also reflect the child-like aspects of me as an adult:

1.   I cannot imagine living without the Other. In fact, a child is so immersed in a relationship with the Other that separate existence is unthinkable.

Needless to say, when I was an infant the "Other" was my mother, Ruth Boyd. Today the "Other" is God.

2.   I completely trust the Other. I am dependent and helpless.

3.   My original environment is the Other. Thus my first experience is being surrounded by a human, rather than an inhuman, environment.[54]

4.   My energy and existence came from the Other, and insofar as I gain independence, it is based on the energy and existence given by the Other as a gift.

5.   I did not know time as an infant. There was no yesterday or tomorrow, only now. This is the quality of the present moment that could be called eternity (John 5:24), or "the eternal now."

6.   I frequently lost my identity in fusion with my mother. Our egos were not separable. There was a mystical union with the Other.

7.   At an early age I didn't believe in the existence of death. I could not even imagine it.

8.   Before age eight months I thought people ceased to exist when I didn't see them, and were resurrected when I saw them again.[55] When I learned the game of "peek-a-boo," I thought it was hilarious that people exist even when I don't see them.

If I am correct that infants think in this way, the implications for understanding the human soul are profound.

I am not saying that Christianity is based on regression, nor does it require regression. What I am saying is that one

of the many benefits of this religion is that it taps into the
child-like resources at the core of our soul. Jesus urged us to
become like little children (Matthew 18:1-5; 19:13-14; Mark
9:33-37; Luke 9:46-48; John 3:1-8):

> He called a child, whom he put among them, and said,
> "Truly I tell you, unless you change and become like
> children, you will never enter the kingdom of heaven."
> (NRSV: Matthew 18:2-3)

Donald Winnicott was the first psychoanalyst to notice
how healthy worship is in terms of evoking the infantile
playfulness of our *psyche*.[56]

I would go beyond Winnicott. I think that my religion
offers me a way of understanding myself and my world, such
that my adult attitudes are brought into alignment with the
infantile core of my soul. The deepest strivings of my soul are
fulfilled by God. Only through religion can I find the full
creativity and playfulness which was so refreshing when I
was an infant.

This view also makes it possible to understand the concept
of "soul murder" (see Chapter 1). The children Rev. Dr. Alan
Broadhead describes in the state mental hospital in North
Dakota had their lives disrupted by sexual and physical abuse
during the first eighteen months of life, when the soul was in
its formative stages. The result of child abuse was the
destruction of the soul before it had become fully organized.
The result of that, decades later, would be a person with no
sense of identity. At the core of such a person, one would
find emptiness or self-loathing. Such a person might not even
have a "self" to loathe.

I think God has a sense of who a person is, even if the
person has no sense of identity and is haunted by emptiness
and worthlessness inside. Thus there would be a divergence
between God's view and the person's own view. My friend
Alan, the psychiatrist-priest, was responding to the child the
way I expect God might respond: with altruism, forgiveness,
generosity, and "justification by faith alone."

As Professor Stendahl has observed, this symbiosis of infancy is evident not only in one's openness to God. It is also evident in one's openness to other people, Christ's second commandment. As Saint Augustine said, "Friendship . . . , too, is a delightful bond, uniting many souls in one."[57]

Pandora's Box

As I said above, we have opened Pandora's Box.

According to my view of the soul, faith is intertwined with a person's psychological makeup. As one person told me, her faith and her psychology are like two threads that are woven together to form the fabric of who she is, and neither thread can be removed without unraveling the entire person. This interplay of the two themes is illustrated in the next chapter.

Chapter 16
One Soul in Depth

Rev. Dr. Alan Broadhead, who spoke to me about "soul murder" in Chapter 1, works five days a week at the state mental hospital as a psychiatrist. On Saturdays and Sundays, he preaches at various parishes in North Dakota as a minister. Why his wife Pat encourages his workaholic tendencies, I don't understand. She seems utterly devoted to him.

A more detailed picture of his life will show how entangled religion and psychiatry are within his soul. They may be distinct disciplines in the external world. But within Alan's life, there is a merging of the religious and psychiatric themes.

Alan's work today is dramatically different than before.

When I first met Alan, he had a prestigious private practice of longterm psychoanalytic psychotherapy in Hartford, Connecticut. Even then, he spent four days a week doing psychiatry and three days a week running a small church in North Branford. But he was dissatisfied with his private practice. His were bright and verbal patients, most of them psychologists, psychiatrists, clergy, lawyers, and psychiatric social workers. For twelve years he had done psychotherapy among the affluent. That should be balanced with twelve years, he thought, working among patients who were indigent and profoundly disturbed.

I know a third person like us: Rev. Dr. John Young, an ordained priest who became a psychiatrist. All three of us work primarily with chronically mentally ill patients who are indigent, the lepers of America. I suspect that ordained clergy who become psychiatrists are attracted toward state mental hospitals like a moth to a flame, because state mental hospitals are where the lepers are.

The last time Alan and I had seen one another, we got angry at one another. It was because back then I thought that psychiatry and religion were different from one another.

"I don't agree with your point of view," Alan had said. "They are the same." In fact, he keeps his practices apart. He does not preach to nor pray with his patients. Nor does he act like a psychiatrist in the sermons I have heard him give.

When I phoned him one day, I was afraid how he might react. I have been fascinated with the man since the moment I met him. When you have the joint training I have, life can be lonely sometimes. I go to church, and people at coffee hour are hesitant to talk to me because I am a psychiatrist. They assume that my X-ray vision will see right through them as if I were Superman. Among psychiatrists, I am considered an odd duck because I believe in expressing my values by working with indigent and grossly psychotic patients.

A Minority Group

We are a minority group within our profession. Only 43% of the members of the American Psychiatric Association and 43% of the American Psychological Association believe in God.[58] By contrast, 94% of the American people believe in God.[59] We also act like a minority group. For example, in my hospital, it has taken five years before other Christians trusted me enough to hint that they also have religious beliefs. They do so furtively and in whispers. I don't advertise my religion, nor do I talk about it. Over five years it has become whispered among the staff:

"Do you know what I heard? I heard that Dr. Boyd is a minister also!"

We are a minority group in that we are sometimes embarrassed about our identity. At least that has been my experience. During the decades when I sought success in academic psychiatry, I frequently succumbed to the temptation to hide the lamp of my priesthood under a bowl (Matthew 5:14-16). It took me a long time to decide I was willing to risk my entire career in academic psychiatry by writing this book.

This minority group of religious professionals is disorganized. We don't communicate with each other, in my experience.

The other day a social worker at my hospital asked me what was the book I was working on. I will call her Karen. I like her a lot, and I think she likes me. After some hesitation, I decided to answer the question. "It's a weird book," I said. "It's about the soul." Karen looked at me in a way she had never looked at me before. "The . . . soul?" she said. She looked horrified and appalled. I got the impression she thought maybe I could infect her with the bubonic plague transmitted through my words. I had not wanted to shock Karen, and regretted having told her about my book.

From my work in the civil rights movement, I have come to believe that the only way for a minority group to feel self-respect is to discard the opinion of the dominant culture, and take some pride in their identity.

Alan has been like an oasis, a comrade. Whether our last parting was slightly irritating because of true differences, or because it had been hard to say goodbye to one another, I didn't know. That was our last conversation before he moved from Connecticut to North Dakota.

He was delighted to hear from me. He reminded me of our previous differences:

"I take the transcendent point of view," Alan said. "Therefore, I tend to see everything as 'one.' In the past, you took more of an immanent point of view. You were more oriented to the world around you, Jeff. When the world told you that psychiatrists and the church are doing different things," he said, "you believed it to be so. I am more schizoid. I don't really care about what the world around me thinks.

Whether other people like me or dislike me doesn't bother
me."

I was relieved that he was so gracious about my having
been a dullard.

Defining "the Soul"

"I have discovered a definition of the word 'soul,'" I told
him. "Your soul is who you are."

"It is the spirit and not the soul that gets my juices
flowing," Alan said. "It was spirit that brought life to the
valley of the dry bones in Ezekiel's vision."

I feel a thrill I feel every time I talk with Alan. It's as if he
brings life to these dry bones of mine.

Something Alan had told me years ago, when he had a
psychotherapy practice, came to mind:

"Most patients in psychotherapy come eventually to
express yearnings for something more, for something that
transcends their immediate situation. That is religion. In
psychotherapy I encourage patients to explore these
yearnings. I don't preach; I don't ever suggest that they
should turn to the Judeo-Christian tradition. Whatever they
find on that quest is fine. But perhaps my practice is unusual;
perhaps spiritually hungry patients seek me out as a
therapist."

Alan experiences psychiatry and religion as doing the
same thing in terms of treating the soul. For example, one
time I went to his church at 7 p.m. on a week night to hear
evening prayer. It was a dark church with a half-dozen
parishioners on their knees. I felt a profound sense of
quietude settle into my soul. The hassle of traffic jams, which
I had experienced moments earlier, vanished. I listened to a
middle-aged woman lead the prayers. Afterwards Alan and I
had dinner.

"Evening prayer is like a small family gathering," he said.
"Six to ten people come, usually the same people every night,
although sometimes someone new will arrive. That woman
who ran the worship service tonight was shy and reticent
five years ago, afraid to say or do anything. Five years ago,

she would have been incapable of speaking in public. She was very bright, but totally intimidated and fearful. I once said to her, 'God gave you a brain; perhaps God meant that you should use it.' Over the last five years in the church, I have watched her grow. It feels like a safe place for her to grow, because it is a small, friendly church. She now runs worship services and is senior warden," i.e. the chief layperson. "She is the best senior warden we ever had."

I find it impossible to argue with Alan. My logical arguments are countered not by logic, but by stories and vignettes. His style of language is the style Jesus used: avoid logical debate and go for the parable. In this story about the woman senior warden, Alan had conveyed his notion that the church is a therapy group, the purpose of which is human growth — soul growth.

"Look," I said, "what you describe is not the kind of religion that most people experience. For most people, religion is oppressive, stifling, encouraging a rigid approach. In fact, I often think that most people would be better off if they discarded their religion."

"Saying we should discard religion is like saying we should discard motherhood," Alan said. "Not all mothers are good mothers. Some are neglectful or abusive. But the fact that some mothers are bad is no reason to discredit all mothers. Other mothers are nurturant, and encourage their children's growth."

His view is that both psychiatry and religion are aimed at human growth in the context of suffering.

"The skill which is required of a really good minister is the same as the skill required of a really good psychotherapist," Alan once told me, "namely the ability to be present to another person in that person's suffering, without defensiveness."

"Psychotherapy is not religion," I had replied. "Psychotherapy has to do with helping people with their problems, not with transcendence." I used the word "transcendence" because I knew it was a buzzword in Alan's vocabulary, meaning "religion."

"It is reductionistic to define psychotherapy as being limited to people's defenses and neuroses," Alan had said. "Everyone in therapy eventually begins to think about the larger issues of life, such as 'Why?' or 'What is the point of my life?' They begin to yearn for transcendence, for something more. You know, I have never met a pure atheist. I have never met a person who thinks that we are just this collection of molecules that comprise the body. No one is satisfied with pure, materialistic self-interest. They may not express it in terms of the Judeo-Christian religion, but everyone has their own private way of making connections between themselves and the transcendent."

You Must Become as Little Children

"I have been thinking," I said, "about the experience of religion. Like me, you find that religion is a matter of a transformed awareness, not just a matter of beliefs. You say that you take the transcendent point of view. You see everything as 'one.' My experience is that worship and prayer induces a state of fusion in which I cannot distinguish between myself and the environment and people around me. My boundaries get blurred. Well, that experience of fusion is exactly what I experienced when I was an infant. I could not distinguish between myself and my mother. We were one and the same. She was my environment, exactly as God is my environment during a worship service. What do you think about the idea that religion taps into that archaic level of our *psyche*? Religion brings my conscious mind into alignment with the most primitive level of my unconscious."

"It certainly makes sense to me," he replied. "As adults we are in a foreign land. I try to think about the physiology of religion."

A conversation with Alan is like setting off for a trip, and immediately taking an unexpected turn and getting lost.

"What?" I asked.

"The Jesus prayer is recited at exactly the same speed as the maternal heart beat," he said.

"What Jesus prayer?" I asked.

"'Jesus Christ, have mercy on me,'" he replied. "This prayer is said over and over again, in a repetitive chant. Sometimes the prayer has a slower rhythm, 'Jesus Christ, son of God, have mercy on me a sinner.' The timing of the words is exactly the timing of the maternal heart beat. It is like a mantra from the Asian religions. A mantra is chanted over and over to induce a sense of transcendence. Well, this is a Christian mantra. Mantras and the Jesus prayer are said at the same speed as a grandfather clock ticks. If you have ever listened to a grandfather clock, it is profoundly relaxing. That's because it goes at the speed of the maternal heartbeat we listened to before we were born. On the other hand, one of those clocks that sits on the mantle goes 'tick-tick-tick-tick,' makes you tense. That's because it is not at the speed of the human heartbeat. I noticed it with my children. They would bond to me, hold onto the edge of my clothing and suck it. They felt the timing of my heartbeat when they put their head on my chest. Worship is comforting, like bonding to your parent when you are an infant. It's what I call the physiology of religion. I don't think this observation undercuts the validity of our faith."

"I never meant to imply that it undercut the validity of our faith," I said.

"No, you didn't," he said. "But that is a question I wrestled with for years. Could it be that faith is an infantile fantasy? Then I realized that it was only natural that our religion would tie into our experience. The early weeks of my life in infancy were imprinted on me forever. It was natural that when God revealed Himself or Herself, that it would be in a way that was familiar to us. In a way that relates to the physiology of the timing of the maternal heartbeat."

Childhood

Disturbing memories came to mind of Alan's description of his childhood. He had a childhood almost as brutal as that of the adolescents described in Chapter 1 who suffered soul murder.

Alan grew up in rural poverty near Manchester, England. His father was a white-collar worker. Timid and meek elsewhere, his father was tyrannical and domineering at home. Alan's father was not physically abusive, but would scream for hours at his wife and child. Loud contentiousness was the usual form of communication at home. Alan's father and mother lived in a destructive symbiotic relationship, Alan said.

His mother never worked outside the house. She was a woman with an abysmal self-regard throughout her life. Were we to meet this woman, she would within three minutes introduce the idea that she had been found as a baby sitting in a gutter, abandoned by her "real" mother. The shame of being illegitimate tortured her. As a reflection of the emotional squalor inside her, as an adult she kept her house filthy, with thick dust and dirt over everything, and stacks of moldy dishes in the sink. When Alan later worked as a doctor, he made thousands of house calls, and only in one or two of those houses did he ever see more filth than that with which he had grown up. He was not taught to wash or bathe. His clothes were wrinkled and smelled badly. Neither manners nor social graces were taught to Alan at home.

Alan was an only child.

"A neglected or abused child holds onto the hope that someday his parents will give him some affection," he said. "It is not a hope based on experience. It is a hope based on fantasy. If the child doesn't have that hope, then the child has nothing at all. On the basis of such hope I was intensely loyal to my parents."

His family had no friends or social life. He carefully avoided telling anyone outside how bad it was at home. Later he discovered that the neighbors all knew. His family was notorious in the neighborhood. Occasionally Alan's paternal grandfather would visit and show interest in Alan. But for the most part, he had no nurturance or caring during the first four years of his life.

He spent most of his time in solitude, and grew comfortable with introverted fantasies. Loving nature, he hiked across the fields and collected bugs and mice. His fantasy life and reverie managed to remain a healthy part of his life, allowing him to survive childhood, and giving him a rich imagination as an adult. He thinks that under circumstances of such severe deprivation and abuse, a child either makes it or fails to make it. This is not based on any decision on the part of the child. It is a matter of the child's constitution, perhaps a genetically determined characteristic. As luck would have it, Alan was one of the children who made it.

"When we speak of an experience of fusion with the environment during worship," I said, "I am reminded of the reverie you experienced as you were playing alone in the fields as a child."

"Yes," he replied. "I have been overwhelmed at times by the majesty of the sea, and the sky, and the sun. It is almost pantheistic. I love the Song of Creation from the *Apocrypha*."

"What is that?" I asked.

"Here it is," he said:

> O ye sun and moon, bless ye the Lord:
>   praise and exalt him above all for ever.
> O ye stars of heaven, bless ye the Lord:
>   praise and exalt him above all for ever.
>
> O every shower and dew, bless ye the Lord:
>   praise and exalt him above all for ever.
> O all ye winds, bless ye the Lord:
>   praise and exalt him above all for ever,
>
> O ye fire and heat, bless ye the Lord:
>   praise and exalt him above all for ever.
> O ye winter and summer, bless ye the Lord:
>   praise and exalt him above all for ever.
>
> O ye dews and storms of snow, bless ye the Lord:
>   praise and exalt him above all for ever.
> O ye nights and days, bless ye the Lord:
>   praise and exalt him above all for ever.

O ye light and darkness, bless ye the Lord:
    praise and exalt him above all for ever.
O ye ice and cold, bless ye the Lord:
    praise and exalt him above all for ever.

O ye frost and snow, bless ye the Lord:
    praise and exalt him above all for ever.
O ye lightnings and clouds, bless ye the Lord:
    praise and exalt him above all for ever.[60]

"Did you have that sense of reverie from the earliest part of your life?" I asked.

"Yes," he said. "From as far back as I can remember."

Internalization of Parents

"Well, where on earth did that originate?" I asked. "You had a pretty awful mother. How could you have this experience of bonding with nature? Did you bond to your mother? Was she the original prototype of Mother Nature? Was your mother nurturant?"

"I have no idea if my mother was nurturant," he replied. "It is not something that I ever remember. On the other hand, the bonding between infant and mother can occur the other way around also. I was a possession of my mother's, like a toy. When I was an infant, I brought joy into her life. As I grew older, she had trouble accepting my independence. She had a hard time giving up breast-feeding me. My independence was not welcome. So I suppose from the earliest months of my life, before I began to get independent, she was nurturant. As I grew older, I lived in terror of this wretched woman. But I always longed for her also."

"She was so tormented," I said. "But I remember what you said about her finding peace in senility in her old age."

"In the last six months of her life," Alan said, "she finally found the serenity which had eluded her all her life. In the eighth decade of life she became demented. Finally, she forgot the bitterness of being an illegitimate child. People said she looked like an angel, she was so tranquil. I wondered if maybe I caught a glimpse then of the angelic mother I knew during the first six months of my life."

"Did you internalize these parents?" I asked him.

"These parent imagos," he said. "Yes. I used to have a punitive and tyrannical superego. That superego came from internalizing my parents. I felt worthless, unacceptable. Only after I went through seven years of psychoanalysis did I come to see what Paul was talking about when he spoke of 'justification by faith alone.' Before psychoanalysis, when I was in seminary, I thought I was justified by good works. I had a primitive superego type of religion. My ability to feel OK based on faith alone was cemented by psychoanalysis. Before psychoanalysis I was dreadfully depressed, sometimes for months at a time. For decades I had a deep inner sense of worthlessness, and intense feelings of rage. I was terribly insecure and shy."

Alan once told me something about God which has haunted me every time I talk with him. He described the "savage indifferent side of God":

"Traditionally God has been experienced in remote and barren places," Alan had said. "On Mount Sinai, in the Himalaya Mountains, in the desert with Jesus. I love the majesty of the Rocky Mountains, or the absolute silence of the Dakota Badlands. Recently I walked for hours through the desert, in the Badlands. There I experienced the side of God which is utterly indifferent to human existence. In the overwhelming emptiness of the desert — which is like walking through the mountains of the moon — I experience the savage indifference of God. It is destructive to one's narcissism. That is why I like to go to remote and barren places."

Somehow, I don't understand how, this experience of God must be part of what Alan felt about his parents as he sat alone in the fields as a small child. My psychiatric intuition tells me that the "savage indifference" that he sometimes feels from God reflects Alan's internalization of bad parents. He has told me that he became schizoid, that he didn't care for the company of people. He describes God almost as if God had a schizoid side. Certainly his parents did.

From this one learns that even a psychiatrist-priest is capable of confusing God with his superego (internalized parents).

Fortunately, that is not the only way that Alan experiences God.

"Were your parents internalized entirely as 'bad parents?'" I asked. "Was there anything positive they gave you?"

"I had a powerful longing for my parents," he replied. "For years I didn't recognize it. Only when I got into psychoanalysis did I realize how much I longed for them. It was why I got so depressed. Like seeing my dad at the end of a long lane. 'Daddy, daddy, daddy,' I would shout, and run down the lane to greet him. Of course, my longing for my father would be destroyed almost immediately by the stupidity of his behavior."

The good internalized parents for Alan are the fantasy parents, the caring parents he wished he had, but didn't. It is sad.

What Saved This Kid?

It would be reasonable to expect that a child like Alan wouldn't have amounted to anything. What happened?

Alan's parents were intensely ambitious for him. They wanted him to achieve everything they had failed to. Never did they go to church, nor were they in any way religious. But for some reason they wanted Alan to join the local church, perhaps in the hope that religion would prevent him from getting interested in sex when he grew to be a teenager. That would have been consistent with Alan's mother's opposition to his growing independence.

There was a mission church in a barn at the other end of the country lane on which they lived. When Alan was four, his parents told him that he should go up to the Mission Church and see what it was like. They did not offer to go with him. If he didn't like it, he need never go back again, they said. So he wandered up the street, a filthy and smelly four-year-old, and found his way into the barn.

What greeted him there was an experience that changed his life permanently.

As luck would have it, it was Feast of the Harvest, the British equivalent of Thanksgiving. He wandered into a place lined wall to wall with fragrant food, home-baked bread and pies, fresh flowers, music, gaiety, and a festive spirit. This being farm country, the Feast of the Harvest was a major feast day. He was welcomed and loved. He adored it. It was like the beginning of real life for him. Suddenly, he had discovered life outside the miserable confines of his home. This little mission church had no minister. Lay readers led the worship services. Once a month, a minister from outside would come by. By other people's standards it was a provincial, backwater, poverty-stricken, tiny place. But for Alan, it became his new home base and the center of his emotional life.

Adults in the church became surrogate parents to Alan. They loved him by virtue of their faith, and by virtue of their membership in the church. For example, there was a man who ran the youth group, which consisted of eight or nine kids. This man, Richard Whitehouse, was not well educated. He was barely a supervisor in his factory. But he would ride his bicycle nine miles through all kinds of weather in order to be there to run the church group, and Alan could absolutely rely on the fact that he would be there, no matter what the weather. It was an impressive demonstration of commitment that was incredibly important to Alan. He learned he could rely on Richard Whitehouse in a way that he had been unable to rely on his parents.

"I sometimes wonder if I would have been such a devoted Christian," Alan said, "if life had been pleasant at home. The church wouldn't have been such a lifesaver had I not been drowning. For example, the other day I was telling my son that he was lucky he didn't have the hard life I had when I was his age. My son said, 'If you really want us to appreciate life, dad, you would have to beat the shit out of us and pretend you don't like us.'"

"You have told me," I said, "that the little mission church in the barn was your 'saving grace.'"

"I internalized the church as my positive parents," Alan replied. "It was because it was right down the street. Had I been raised in Palestine, there would have been a mosque down the street, and I would have internalized the mosque. I would have become a devout Moslem. That is why I think that Christians and Jews, Moslems and Buddhists are equal. It all depends what is down the street."

"Did you internalize Richard Whitehouse?" I asked.

"Yes, he became part of my hagiography," Alan replied.

"Hagiography?" I asked.

"One of the saints whose name is carved in my mind," he said. "I call these introjections imagos. Fortunately, the people I met were those who cared about other people. Richard Whitehouse really cared about others, and not just to serve his own self-interest. So I introjected people like him. Therefore, I learned to care about other people. It is why I am not just the solitary, schizoid person I was during the first four years of my life. I was just lucky. If I had been Oliver Twist I might have introjected Fagin, and then I would have grown up to be a thief. It is just a matter of luck that the people I met as a child were caring, and not Fagin."

The word "introjected" means internalizing the other person — making a psychological model inside your mind of what another person is like. The "introject" then becomes part of your psychological makeup.

"I am struck," I said, "with how you approach church school in your church now that you are a middle aged minister."

"Church school is of vital importance," Alan said. "I tell my church school teachers that it is not important whether or not the children learn the facts of the faith. I don't care if the children never heard of the Lord's Prayer or the Ten Commandments. What is important is that the children enjoy coming to church school. This is determined by the emotional bond between student and teacher. If church school is a rewarding experience, then the children will continue to attend, and the church will have an entire lifetime in which to teach them the facts of the religion. But if they don't enjoy coming, then they will drop away from the church. Therefore,

I stress that the teachers must find a way to know and like each child. I don't care whether they stick to lesson plans."

"What also strikes me," I said, "is that religion opened your horizons. People sometimes speak to me as if Christianity advocates provincialism and a narrow-minded approach. Yet my own experience is that I was provincial and narrow minded as an atheist. I was converted to Christianity. The religion was a cosmopolitan influence for me."

"The only outside speakers who ever came to this out-of-the-way corner of the earth," Alan said, "were missionaries from China and Africa and other exotic places. They would bring fanciful clothes for us kids to try on. They talked about places that were very different than this little farming village which was my whole experience. My imagination would soar. I began to formulate a plan. I wanted to be a minister because I wanted to give something to the church, in exchange for all that the church had given me. And specifically I wanted to be a missionary, and go to someplace fabulous and exotic. To this end I thought it might be neat to become a doctor, a medical missionary."

"And now," I said, "your dream has come true."

"You are right," Alan replied. "Here I have found everything I ever wanted as a child. I am a medical missionary in an exotic place, North Dakota."

"Did Jesus become internalized," I asked, "similar to the way your parents and Richard Whitehouse did?"

"Life is tragic and terribly hard," Alan said. "The human lot is to suffer from hardships, tragedy, and to have difficulty with intimate emotional relationships. The challenge is to grow and blossom in such arid soil. The only kind of religion that makes a difference is to experience either that another person is present with me in my suffering, or that Jesus is present with me in my suffering. Jesus is in the same boat as me, and quelling the storm of my emotions, bringing a peace that passes all understanding. Jesus is a friend who suffered as much as I suffered, and who triumphed over that suffering by his victory on the cross."

The False Self

I decided to change the subject.

"It seems to me that there is a false self, or false identity," I said. "Does that make sense to you?"

This question arose from my theory of the soul. If my soul is who I truly am, there might be a divergence between that and who I think I am. The latter would be called a "false self" or "false identity."[61]

"No," Alan replied. "I don't understand what you mean."

"It is the mask I show the world," I said, "but may be estranged from whom I really am."

"I don't know what you are talking about," he said. "People sometimes see only one facet of me. Is that what you mean? Like when I used to get depressed so much, before psychoanalysis, I didn't let people see that depressed side of me."

"Well, sort of," I said. I was frustrated.

"Why is this an important question to you, Jeff?" he asked.

"Look, I think of my soul as being the person I really am," I said, "in the eyes of God."

"In the eyes of God?" he asked.

"Do you think we can know how God views us?" I asked.

"We can know God only as God chooses to reveal Himself or Herself," he replied. "If you believe Scripture, it is clear that God is responsive and generous. In the parable of the pearl of great value, it is we who are the pearl of great value, and it is God who longs for us. In the Scripture about the lilies of the field, God is taking care of our every need. So I would say, yes, we can know something of the mind of God. Because God reaches out to us and tells us what we need to know."

"Well," I said, "if my soul is the person God knows me to be, then that might be quite different from the person I think I am. That is what I call my 'false self.' In other words, the 'false self' is my erroneous idea of who I am, based on lies and rationalizations. It is perhaps the part that is successful in the world but is not who God really knows me to be."

"Look, Jeff," Alan said, "you have a *curriculum vitae* that radiates brilliance. By comparison with you, I feel inadequate." This comment surprised me. I have often felt inferior to Alan. "I don't have such a scintillating *curriculum vitae*," Alan said. "You've graduated from places like Brown, Harvard, Yale, and the National Institute of Mental Health. That's why I think this idea of the 'false self' is important to you and not to me. You have been to the top, and you know that it doesn't work. You have learned from experience that success in the world does not bring fulfillment in life. Intellectually, I know that also. But inside I am always a little insecure. I keep thinking that maybe if I had gone to Oxford-Cambridge, that my life on earth would be more rewarding. You know from first-hand experience that it isn't. I don't have that experience. Recently some friends I knew in England, who had been to Oxford-Cambridge, became bishops. I have the fantasy that those guys have the perfect life. Actually, I know that they are probably riddled with doubts, and have emotional and marital conflicts just like anyone else. But emotionally I keep thinking if my life had simply gone better, then perhaps I would be truly happy. My experience of life is that of constantly searching for that which I don't have but which I think someone with a better *curriculum vitae* does have. Your experience of life, Jeff, is probably one of disappointment. You have tried to pursue success in the world, and you have achieved it, and you find it disappointing. You know from experience that the rewards of the world aren't rewarding. I always hope that they might be."

"So the idea of a 'false self' doesn't make any sense in your experience of life?" I was disappointed in my theory.

"Well, perhaps it does," he conceded. "I have always tended to regard myself as a country bumpkin. My false self is the idea, 'I can't do this because I'm just a country bumpkin.' It is not who I really am. But it is how I often present myself."

I was relieved that my theory of the "false self" made some sense to him. My image of Alan is incompatible with a "country bumpkin."

Evangelical Christians

"The 'false self' describes some of the evangelical Christians I have treated in my psychiatry practice," Alan volunteered. "They were extremely rigid people. They held tightly to a form of Christianity which seemed to defend them from reality, rather than one which opened them up to reality. Their religion was a paranoid worldview according to which life was simple, unambiguous, full of black-and-white moral decisions. They were convinced of the certitude of their perspective."

"That isn't your approach," I commented.

He became adamant: "We Christians have long said that doubt is part of faith. We have long said that faith is not certainty. We have long said that faith is a leap into the darkness."

"I think there are some strengths to the evangelical approach," I said. "I know a woman with borderline personality disorder who was cured by that kind of religion. I think you are being judgmental. I don't agree with you."

Alan was unconvinced. "Religious conservatives are trying to make human nature into something that it is not. The correct approach, I think, is to recognize that human nature, as it is, is sacred, and to try to reveal what human nature really is. There is something forced about a moralistic approach to religion. I seek to discover the divine in the midst of human nature. I think that theology has to be built from the bottom up, not from the top down. Theology must begin with ordinary human experience. Psychotherapy challenges one to recognize the complexity, ambiguity, threat, hidden meanings, contradictions, and subtlety of life. Psychotherapy challenges one to take ownership of disowned ideas. It challenges one to stop taking such a defensive stance in life and to look honestly at whatever it is one is afraid of."

Although I disagreed with Alan about evangelical Christians, I bit my tongue, wanting to hear him out.

"There is a strong sense of anger and a judgmental attitude radiating from the evangelical Christians," Alan continued. "This is very different from what I find in the presence of truly holy people, such as monks who have devoted their life to God, and who are clearly more advanced than me in terms of spiritual journey. Truly holy people radiate a sense of peace and acceptance of life, and an acceptance of me. It is at the same time loving and it inspires me to grow spiritually. By contrast, evangelical Christians make me feel uncomfortable because of the hidden rage. It is not a rage which is explicit. On the surface, these people are often humble and friendly. They believe that they have the truth, and that God is condemning you since you do not have the truth. They believe that God is angry at most people in the world and is condemning them to Hell. Therefore they don't have to take responsibility for that anger. They can experience themselves as completely loving, and allow God to be the one who is full of anger and rage."

"I still disagree with you about evangelical Christians," I said. "I think you are speaking in stereotypes. Furthermore, I think you are barking up the wrong tree. Whether the evangelicals think of God as being an angry God who passes judgment is irrelevant. The question is whether the New Testament portrays God that way. I think the New Testament does say that! Furthermore, if you criticize them for being so judgmental, then how come you are so judgmental toward them? You complain too loudly of the speck of sawdust in your brother's eye."

Alan and I never saw eye to eye on this subject.

Clergy

"What about the clergy you have treated as patients?" I asked. "Do they have a 'false self?'"

"Most clergy are highly motivated, honest, and sincere, in my experience," Alan said. "They are placed in an impossible situation by the church. They often think of themselves as being neurotic. Actually they are not the source of the problem, their job is. A highly educated and motivated clergy-person is put in a leadership position with uneducated lay people who have a rigid approach and a distorted sense of what is important. Sometimes stupid, picayune details will seem crucial to vestry members, which is frustrating.

"America is known as the land of religious fervor," Alan continued, "but that is no longer true. Today the primary experience in churches is that of religious monotony. People come to church for the sake of their children. When their children go off to college, the parents stop coming. I ran into one of my former church leaders in the grocery store. He and his wife scurried off down a side aisle of the store to avoid me. They had stopped coming to church after their youngest child went off to college. It hurt my feelings."

"Don't the clergy have a 'false self' in terms of being moralistic and judgmental?" I asked.

"Usually the clergy are not judgmental," Alan said, "but the public expects them to be. The public acts as if the clergy represented their own superego. There is something very adolescent about the way people treat clergy. Parishioners tell the minister half the truth but not the other half of the truth. That's because they expect a moralistic and judgmental response. They don't give the clergy-person the advantage that they give to a psychiatrist."

"What advantage?" I asked.

"Telling both sides of the truth," he said. "For example, a patient may have a conflict between the wish to have a sexual affair and a moral conviction that forbids it. Psychiatrists want to hear both sides of the conflict. Therefore, they don't take sides. They don't want the patient to disown the lust. And they don't want the patient to disown the moral feelings. In our culture, people are more honest with psychotherapists than with the clergy. Many patients have told me that they feel free to say things to me that they have never told anyone else. There is almost a confessional quality to many therapy sessions. If they discover that I am a clergyman, they are often horrified. 'Oh my God,' they say, 'I would never have told you about having an affair if I had known you were a clergyman!'"

"I agree, yet I also disagree," I said. "My experience is that patients aren't all that honest with me as a psychiatrist, at least with respect to their faith. In my practice of psychiatry, I don't advertise that I am ordained. Patients come to me and talk very little about religion. When a few do talk about religion, they might describe Christianity as guilt-inducing. The impression I get is that Christianity is psychologically unimportant, or sometimes destructive. But then some of these patients subsequently hear a rumor in the community that I am ordained. The same patients who previously had nothing to say about religion now begin to talk with excitement about how emotionally helpful prayer and God have been, helping them to restore their psychological balance, as it says in Psalm 23:3, 'God restores my soul.' Thus my experience is that people distort the truth as much when they talk with psychotherapists as when they talk to clergy. But they distort different aspects of the truth. With the clergy they may lie about sexual affairs. With psychothera-pists they avoid talking about their faith. Neither group of professionals knows that they are hearing only part of the truth."

Satan

"By the way," I changed the subject, "what is your view of Satan? Is there not a malignant influence on our soul?"

"Funny you should ask," he said. "North Dakota is the satanic capital of the United States. One of our churches was vandalized and a fire lit on the altar. There are no suspects. It is assumed to be the work of this satanic cult."[62]

"That is not what I am asking about," I said. "I want to know about your personal experience."

"I have always believed there is one God and not two gods," he said. "That there is a god of evil doesn't make sense to me. On the other hand, I do believe there are demonic pressures or powers in life. The evangelicals speak of 'deliverance.' They talk about 'deliverance from the power of evil.' I think they are too concrete. I can't imagine Satan being a person with a personality. If the evangelicals would be less concrete, I could agree with them. I think we are at a crossroads. There is a battle of good and evil on earth, and we are at a crossroads. We have to choose which way to go."

"Can you give me an example of what you mean?" I asked.

"Many patients in longterm therapy are tortured by some memory of how another person injured them," Alan said. "There is an urge for retribution during a divorce. There is revenge toward an unfaithful spouse. A Jewish father whose daughter marries a Roman Catholic may hate his daughter. Perhaps a woman was raised in a family that treated her as a second class citizen, while her brother was given all the attention and encouragement. Patients sometimes become very interested in retaliation. And they might feel better if they got revenge. I ask them to consider what are the fantasies which underlie this revenge theme. The underlying fantasies are usually that the opponent will be killed, ground into dust, obliterated. I ask whether the patient won't feel less human if these fantasies are pursued. Would the delight in punishment have a dehumanizing effect, leaving them bitter and angry, I ask. The patient may challenge me: 'So, do you expect me to forgive?'"

"What do you say to that?" I asked.

"I say no," Alan replied.

"But you don't mean it?" I asked.

"No, I don't mean it," he replied. "I ask what effect it would have on the patient's life to pursue the pleasure of revenge. Is it not likely to destroy the patient and everyone else? Can the patient continue to be a real person and emotionally vibrant unless he or she dares to give up the anger and forgives the other person? The answer, in my experience, is clear. Forgiveness is necessary for one's own psychological health."

"So those are the two roads," I said.

"That is the crossroads," he replied.

Conclusion

"Thank you for talking with me," I said. "I always find our friendship rewarding."

"It is a strange friendship," Alan said. "All you do is ask questions. All I do is answer them. I hope it helps you."

"You are very helpful," I said. "Actually I think of you as being like that guy you mentioned from IBM."

IBM once made a survey of its top executives to try to discover what they had in common, Alan had told me. They found great diversity, with nothing in common except ambition. Then they made a fortuitous discovery that a surprisingly large number of the top executives had started in the same small department of the company. They had the same man as a mentor. They had discovered their leadership potential under that man's teaching, and had subsequently gone on to rise through the ranks to the top of the corporate ladder. This humble man had a talent for seeing the unique talents and potential in each employee, and encouraging the employee to cultivate his strengths and not be disabled by his vulnerabilities. This man provides a model for how Alan sees his work both as a therapist and as a minister. This is a model that explains why psychotherapy and ministry are both dealing with the same thing, human potential, using different metaphors. The corporate mentor is also a metaphor for Jesus of Nazareth, in Alan's way of thinking.

"Jesus was an unknown carpenter who died at age thirty-three in an underdeveloped country," Alan said, "who inspired a handful of uneducated fishermen so that they went on to change the entire world."

I felt like one of the fishermen trained by Alan.

"That's very flattering," Alan said, "that you think of me like that executive from IBM. Actually I think of myself more like the fool."

"The fool?" I asked.

"In medieval times there was a role in society called the fool," Alan explained. "The fool was fiercely protected and loved by the community. He was the person who could get away with saying anything, such as mocking the king for the king's stupidity or injustice. The role of the fool captures the essence of Jesus Christ. In his time Jesus served the role of the fool in Israel. He spoke the truth. He mocked the social order. Jesus was fiercely loved by common folk and considered a fool by those who were sophisticated. The fact that he allowed himself to be crucified proved to them that he was a fool (Matthew 27:27-31,39-44; Mark 15:16-20; 16:29-32; Luke 23:35-38). Even afterwards they continued to regard him as a fool (Matthew 28:11-15). Paul said that people expect God to be impressive, but Jesus Christ was not impressive. He said, 'We proclaim Christ crucified, a stumbling block to Jews and foolishness to Gentiles . . . . God's foolishness.' (NRSV: 1 Corinthians 1:23-25). I, like the fool, am an outsider. I understand human suffering. I am available as a friend."

Chapter 17
The "Soul" and Sigmund Freud

The idea that Sigmund Freud was treating part of, but not all of, the "soul" would be implied by any concept of the "soul" which took that word to refer to "who you are." Yet in view of Freud's notorious atheism, it might appear impossible to build a bridge between the concept of the "soul" and Sigmund Freud. This chapter proposes to build such a bridge.

This chapter is not predicated on the assumption that Freud's theories have validity. Even if one finds them to lack all validity, nevertheless one must admit that Freud attempted to treat the personality and/or the whole person of his patients. Questions of Freud's validity aside, Freud was walking on the same territory as the word "soul" refers to, as even Karl Barth said.[63]

There would be two ways to build a bridge: from Freud to the concept of the "soul," or vice versa. The first approach will be shown to be futile. The second approach will be shown to be successful when we consider Freud's close friend Pastor Oskar Pfister.

First Approach

Bruno Bettelheim, M.D., wrote an article and a book to the effect that Freud understood his entire life work as bein about the soul.[64] Bettelheim claimed that James Strachey systematically mistranslated Freud's works into English (the *Standard Edition*), avoiding the word "soul."

Rather than trusting Bettelheim, I went back to the original text, and rendered my own translation from German. In 1905 Freud published an article called "Treatment of the Psyche (Treatment of the Soul)" [German: *Psychische Behandlung (Seelenbehandlung)*].[65] It reads:

> *Psyche* is a Greek word and translates into German as "soul" (German: *Seele*). Treatment of the *psyche* means therefore treatment of the soul (*Seelenbehandlung*). One could also understand it to mean treatment of sickness when it occurs in the life of the soul (*Seelenlebens*). This, however, is not the only meaning of these words. Treatment of the *psyche* means more than this. It means treatment arising from the soul (*Seele*), treatment of disturbances of the soul (*seelischer*) or body, with methods which first and immediately concern the soul (*Seelische*) of people.

A German-English dictionary shows that Bettelheim is right: "soul" is the most accurate translation of *Seele*.[66] James Strachey translated *Seele* as "mind" in this passage.[67] That was misleading, but not totally wrong.

The Greek *psyche* translates as "soul" not only in German, but also in English. Rich words like this could be translated other ways also, but the main translation would be "soul."

Having said this, I have proved little. Even if Freud intended the word *psyche* to refer to the "soul," what did he mean by that latter term? He never defined it. Bettelheim may be correct that Freud chose words like "soul" and *psyche* that evoked a mysterious and turbulent meaning inside the minds of his German speaking audience.

Let us recall the goal of this chapter, to demonstrate that Freud's *psyche* was part of, but not all of, the "soul." Because the biblical term "soul" existed in the context of a relationship with God, and Freud was an atheist, we can see that he certainly did not intend the theological implications of the word. The idea of an immortal *psyche* would have been alien to Freud. Nor would he have appreciated the idea of a resurrected *psyche*.

Second Approach:
Pastor Oskar Pfister

I started with Freud, and tried to build a bridge to the biblical "soul." It comes as no surprise that this effort failed. After all, Freud was an atheist. What may surprise many is how easy it is to build a bridge from the "soul" to Freud. Pastor Oskar Pfister was a Lutheran minister in Zürich, who adored Sigmund Freud.[68] By the way, although Pfister was from Zürich, he had no warm feelings toward Carl Jung. When they first met, Freud warned Pfister that psychoanalysis could destroy Pfister's Christian faith. Pfister decided he wanted to be psychoanalyzed by Freud, because if his faith was based on an illusion, better he should know it. By the end of the psychoanalysis, Pfister's faith was as robust as ever.

Pfister was somewhat younger than Freud, and idolized the master, somewhat replacing his dead father with Freud. For thirty years these two had an affectionate, warm, and mutually respectful relationship. There is a whole book of letters they wrote back and forth. They defined religion as one of the topics about which they disagreed. Freud tended to emphasize the disagreements, whereas Pfister emphasized the compatibility.

For example, he told Freud that Freud was one of the best "Christians" he ever met.[69] According to Pfister, the problem with Freud was that he had grown up around obsessive-compulsive and pathological forms of religion, and had never been exposed to the freedom of true religion.[70] Freud could never figure out how Pfister could be so religious and yet so wonderful.[71]

In his church, Pfister used psychoanalysis as his method of pastoral counseling; an entire psychoanalysis took only three months back in those days. The man whom Freud called "dear man of God," found psychoanalysis was helpful in terms of education of young people. He applied psychoanalytic insights to Christian education. In time he became a mentor of Anna Freud, encouraging her interest in children, and nurturing her career as the first child psychoanalyst. Sigmund Freud, who always felt generous toward Pfister, said child psychoanalysis was "initiated" by Pfister.[72]

When other of Freud's followers visited the home of Sigmund and Martha, the visitors were somewhat stuffy and aloof as viewed through the eyes of Freud's children. But they always looked forward to Pfister, whom Anna described as being like the Pied Piper in terms of his ability to delight and enchant Freud's children.[73]

This man, who quietly and humbly took care of people behind the scenes, was aghast when his countryman Hermann Rorschach died without publishing his great work. Rorschach was one of Freud's followers. Pfister gathered Rorschach's manuscripts and got them published.[74] Without Pfister we would never have heard of Rorschach's ink blot test.

Pfister wrote the first textbook of psychoanalysis, *The Psychoanalytic Method*.[75] He was a prolific writer, and Freud wrote prefaces to some of his books. For example, Freud wrote in one that he had a high regard for the work of Protestant ministers such as Pfister.[76] Why is this news? Because the prefaces to Pfister's books were not published in Strachey's 24-volume set, *The Complete Psychological Works of Sigmund Freud*. The letters Freud exchanged with many other people were included, as were the prefaces Freud wrote for other people's books. The so-called *Complete Psychological Works* are not complete because the influence of Pfister has been edited out.

Soon I will relate how Pfister had a decisive influence on the course of history, in terms of the mental health movement.

First, let me say that Pfister has been largely forgotten. No graduate student in seminary has ever written his biography or summarized his theology. Pfister's works are not read. Fortunately, he has not been completely forgotten. The American Psychiatric Association and the American Mental Health Clergy Association jointly sponsor the annual Oskar Pfister Award.

Here we have a paradox, that Pfister has been largely forgotten although he changed the course of history, was one of Freud's closest friends, and was one of the original twelve disciples of Freud. The way I understand this paradox is that it reflected Pfister's self-concept. He was a humble man whose purpose was to serve God, not to make a name for himself. And that is what he accomplished. He served God, and left not much of a name.

"Illusion of a Future"

Having introduced the man, I will now introduce the bridge he built connecting the biblical idea of "soul" to Freud's term *psyche*.

It was probably the fundamentalists in Tennessee who got Freud enraged. In 1925 they brought to trial a young biology teacher named John Scopes, who was accused of teaching the Darwinian as opposed to the biblical theory of creation. He was found guilty of violating the Butler Act of Tennessee. The case was appealed to the Tennessee Supreme Court in 1927. Meanwhile, the trial made headlines read in Vienna by Freud. Denouncing Darwin in front of Freud would be like throwing raw meat in front of an Alaskan husky.

Freud said he was appalled at the Scopes Monkey Trial.[77] That was precisely when he wrote and published *Future of an Illusion*.[78] In the booklet he made the typical Enlightenment assumption that religion was the enemy of science, and that the former was diminishing while the latter was gaining in importance.

Before publishing *Future of an Illusion*, Freud wrote to apologize to Pfister for having written such a booklet. He indicated that he would have written it years earlier had he not had such respect for Pfister.[79] In his typical style, Pfister wrote back that he found nothing offensive nor startling in Freud's essay. Pfister responded as if to say, "So what else is new?"

In his gracious and somewhat humorous manner, Pfister offered to write a rebuttal. He suggested that it be called "Illusion of a Future," because he wanted to poke fun at this

Enlightenment idea that this fallen world is getting better and better because of science. Freud was delighted with the suggestion.[80] Freud indicated that psychoanalysis was neither pro- nor anti-religion. The religious neutrality of psychoanalysis could be demonstrated to the world by having one of his closest friends publish a rebuttal in the leading psychoanalytic journal, *Imago*, Freud said.[81]

Pfister then produced one of the great documents of Christian literature, a carefully reasoned rebuttal of Freud's *Future of an Illusion*. I will recount momentarily what this document said about the "soul." First, let me point out the tremendous impact this essay had.

To begin with, it changed Freud's way of thinking. The next time he wrote on religion, in *Civilization and Its Discontents*, Freud was much more respectful. For example, he said he admired people whose sophisticated religion places love as the highest value in human life.[82] That had been one of Pfister's main points in "Illusion of a Future." Freud drew a distinction between the few sophisticated people who have a healthy form of religion, and the great masses who are oppressed by the stupidity of their religion. He challenged people like Pfister to recognize that ordinary religion, as practiced by most people, violates this commandment: "Thou shalt not take the name of the Lord thy God in vain."[83] Freud said that!

In *Civilization and Its Discontents* Freud also said, ." . . only religion can answer the question of the purpose of life. One can hardly be wrong in concluding that the idea of life having a purpose stands and falls with the religious system."[84] Here I detect a suggestion that Freud may have been a bit jealous or admiring of Pfister. Freud may have thought Pfister had something valuable that Freud didn't have: a sense of purpose.

Freud then threw down a challenge which our civilization has struggled with throughout the Twentieth Century. He said that most people don't care about the purpose of life. What they care about is being happy.[85] What thwarts human happiness is the oppressive superego inside us.

Freud published that idea in 1929, and it has affected our civilization for the last six decades.

I don't want to overstate the case vis-a-vis Pfister's impact on Freud. Freud remained a convinced atheist. In some of his later works, Freud reverted to a hackneyed form of atheism as if he had never been taught by Pfister.[86]

But more important, Pfister profoundly changed the way all psychoanalysts thought. No one after Freud had the audacity to write that religion was a neurosis in disguise. Leading psychoanalysts such as Erich Fromm wrote books demonstrating that religion and psychoanalysis can be friends.[87] Fromm even called psychoanalysts "physicians of the soul."[88]

Freud's view of religion is strikingly different than the official position of the mental health movement today. Even if there is sometimes a subtle bias against "religiosity" in the mental health field, nevertheless the official position is one of neutrality, which contradicts Freud's *Future of an Illusion*. The best selling book published by the American Psychiatric Association Press in 1986 was pro-religion.[89]

We must ask how it happened that Freud's view did not prevail within the mental health field. Why is it that everyone in the field today believes religion is outside the boundary of their expertise? Why is it that no one in the mental health field ever quotes *Future of an Illusion*? The answer appears to be because of the man of God, who was present at the crucial moment. In the duel between *Future of an Illusion* and "Illusion of a Future," it was Pfister's article which won the future.

Yet surprisingly, it has never been translated into English. W. W. Meissner published some fragments — less than a quarter of it.[90] Ted Crump and I have translated it. It is printed as an appendix to this book.

Pfister's Views on the Soul

I come finally to the central task of this chapter, which is to show how Pfister's view of the soul relates to Freud's *psyche* and to the biblical idea of the "soul."

The question before us is simple. Does Oskar Pfister's essay (see Appendix A) provide a bridge between the biblical concept of the "soul" and Sigmund Freud's concept of the *psyche*?

Let us start with the first half. I claim that Pfister's use of the word "soul" is fairly close to the biblical concept. He used the term to mean the whole person, as in "suffering souls." Souls suffered from illness and required redemption and/or cure. In Pfister's essay the concepts of redemption and cure got somewhat mixed together.**** The soul was something of enormous value; therefore, one would not stake it on an illusion. There were other realities, known only to the soul, and not evident through the five senses. These realities I presume were known to Pfister but not to Freud. Just as spirits enter the soul at various places in the Bible, similarly Pfister found in the unseen realities the source of the soul's excitement.

In the essay, Pfister criticized Freud at some length for Freud's naivete about philosophy. For example, Freud tended to believe in the senses as the source of knowledge, whereas Pfister thought nothing could be known except through the organization of our soul. Pfister chided Freud as being ignorant of the philosophical debates about the concepts that Freud adopted uncritically as if they were scientific fact. (Pfister was more trained in philosophy than was Freud.)

Pfister recognized the soul in the quality of humility preached by Freud. Yet, there was a difference between what Jesus said about bearing our cross, and what Freud said about accepting our fate. Pfister seemed to recognize that it was more noble to bear one's cross with the dignity provided by religion than without that dignity. Atheists, enduring misery with humility, sometimes put a bullet through their head in despair, he said.

**** Krister Stendahl points out that Pfister's confusion of redemption and cure probably reflects Pfister's awareness of the Greek New Testament. The Greek word *sōzō* referred to both salvation and healing. Thus, according to Stendahl, a verse that says "Their faith saved them," could also be translated "Their faith healed them."

Pfister's trump card was to claim the entire realm of artistic creation on behalf of the soul. Science had not inspired artists as had religion. The mental health movement has always tended to view religion as shackling people's souls with guilt. Pfister's response was that guilt was not all there was to religion. Religion brought grace, which liberated our soul from guilt. He also said there was another form of soul enslavement, which the mental health movement did not understand. As long as our horizons are restricted to this earth, our soul is weighted down with countless worries. Religion lifts our soul to the mountaintops, and opens vistas we never imagined.

In conclusion, I claim that Pfister used the word "soul" in harmony with a biblical sense of that word. This is not surprising, considering he was a preacher, first and foremost.

Pfister and Freud's *Psyche*

The last remaining task is to show an organic connection between Pfister's use of the word "soul," and Freud's use of the word *psyche*. Pfister described "psychoanalysis as an instrument by means of which suffering souls cut through their fetters and prison gates are opened, so that they can hasten into the sunshine." This sentence referred to the liberating effect of psychoanalysis. He himself may have experienced this in his analysis with Freud. Freud had a monistic view of the *psyche*, much like the Hebrew word *nephesh* and similar to Pfister's use of the word "soul" in the sentence just quoted. [*Editor's note: "Monistic" means that the human being is viewed as an indivisible whole, not fractured into a soul which is a different substance than the body.*]

Pfister also said, "How finely Jesus practices psychoanalysis 1900 years before Freud!"

Pfister spoke of Freud as having a "soul microscope." Again, this was a clear allusion to *Psycho*-analysis. What Freud referred to as the treatment of the *psyche*, Pfister spoke of as the "cure of souls."

Pfister's discussion about windows of the soul directly parallels Freud's writings about sense organs and erogenous zones which, in his early writings, Freud considered crucial in the development of the *psyche*. Pfister's reply to Freud about the sources of information about "reality" is, in essence, "There are more things in heaven and earth, Horatio, than are dreamt of in your philosophy."

Implicit in Pfister's essay was a decisive dispute. Freud taught that there were two principles inside the *psyche*, the "reality principle" and the "pleasure principle." The former was realistic and allowed us to adapt to realities which were often unpleasant. The latter was childish, unrealistic, self-serving, but was also the source of life's pleasures.

Freud's entire booklet *Future of an Illusion* attempted to classify religion under the rubric of the "pleasure principle." Pfister challenged Freud to enter a debate about what is real. Is God real? Is resurrection real? Are spiritual realities real? Pfister knew that Freud had no possible reply to such a challenge, because psychoanalysis was not competent to define what was real and unreal. If one expanded the "reality principle" to include spiritual realities, then one would re-define the "reality principle" in a style compatible with Pfister and incompatible with Freud's atheism.

Summary

The theme throughout this book is that psychiatrists treat the soul, but that the soul is larger and more paradoxical than psychiatrists know. In this chapter we can see that the "soul" of which Oskar Pfister spoke is larger than, and totally includes, every aspect of the *psyche* of which Freud spoke.

Pfister loved both Jesus Christ and Sigmund Freud, a man whom he described as having "greatness of soul." He showed us the way across the bridge from the soul to Freud and back to the soul. Pfister endorsed Freud's methods for their therapeutic efficacy. But he indicated that the soul was much greater, richer, and more creative than anything Freud ever knew about. True freedom of the soul, Pfister said, cannot be known through psychoanalysis alone. Both psychoanalysis and religion shared a common goal: "the cure of souls."[91]

In addition to his brilliant scholarship, Pfister also took care of the souls in the Freud family — Sigmund, Martha, Anna, and the other children whose names most of us have forgotten: Martin, Mathilde, Oliver, Sophie, and Ernst. Pfister also cared for Sigmund's soul. He scolded Freud for being too pessimistic all the time. Their affection was so strong that Freud was willing to listen to such criticism from his close friend.[92]

The Lord will not suffer the **soul** of the righteous to famish.

(KJV: Proverbs 10:3)

The Lord does not let the righteous go hungry.

(NRSV: Proverbs 10:3)

Chapter 18
Comment by Krister Stendahl

"I can see," said Stendahl, "that you feel called to redeem this word. Your commitment to redeeming the word 'soul' is impressive. The 'soul' that biblical scholars reject is the Platonic 'soul,' not the biblical 'soul.'

"Your whole book," he continued, "is based on thinking things together. You stress the oneness, the unity. Humans are called a 'soul,' which is a unified view of human nature. Your book also says there is this symbiosis of the soul and God.

"Human knowledge knows by distinguishing things," he said. "Western culture has had enormous success in solving problems by distinguishing. This is best illustrated by a double-blind placebo trial in medical research, which is able to distinguish the effects of a drug from those of a placebo. But in your book you go in the opposite direction. Instead of dividing things into parts, you bring the parts together into a unity.

"In Genesis 2:7 there is a unity of the human and the divine," Stendahl said. "This splits apart in Genesis 3, the Fall. In Mary's womb it comes together again. In Jesus Christ we learn how God is most divine when God is most human; that is the paradox of Christian theology.

"Which brings me to the last chapter," he said, "where you draw a distinction between psychiatry and religion. I think this book would end better if that distinction were not that sharp. Psychiatry is found in Christianity, and vice-versa. You and Dr. Alan Broadhead are whole people. You are not psychiatrists and priests. The same person is found in both roles. Wouldn't it be true to say that when you celebrate Communion and serve the bread and wine, that you are present there at the altar with all your psychiatric knowledge and expertise?"

"Yes," I said, "it is true."

"So you are one being — there are not two distinct sides of you?" Stendahl asked.

"Yes," I replied.

"It is like what I teach the clergy about visiting in the hospital," he said. "A patient will say, 'Do you come as a friend or as a priest?' And the answer must be, 'Your friend is a priest, and this priest is your friend.' No split personalities, please!"

Self-Seeking and Attachment

Stendahl referred to Chapter 15:

> Faith does not encourage self-seeking. Even soul-seeking is alien to faith. Faith is not a quest for my identity. It is a quest for God. Faith means living as if God could be trusted.

"I think that is excellent!" Stendahl said. "By the way, have you thought about Buddha at all?"

"Yes, of course," I replied. "Buddha taught that there is no soul — the doctrine called *anātman*."[93]

"Buddha taught," Stendahl said, "that the source of pain and evil is attachment. Now there you have a striking example of a religion which intensifies the insight of monotheism to the Nth Degree. Buddhism is far more monotheistic than is Islam. Islam teaches one should be attached to nothing other than God. Buddhism teaches that one must be attached to nothing, not even to God. One should not even be attached to one's self, one's soul. That is why there is this doctrine of 'no soul.' Of course, when one talks to a Buddhist master and he says there is no soul, what is truly striking is that you can see in his manner how profoundly he is a soul."

"Can you restate what you mean about Buddhism?" I asked.

"One should love God for God's sake, not for what God gives us," Stendahl said. "Luther said there is a kind of religious selfishness, a focus on God saving oneself. The Buddha taught that nothing is absolute but God: not even my attachment to God is absolute.

"Enlightenment is not a name for God," he continued. "There is a difference between salvation and enlightenment. Buddha did not teach salvation because salvation can imply that we are attached to ourselves and to our salvation. But enlightenment means simply that one stands in the light. One is totally lost in the light."

I found Stendahl's comments about Buddhism astonishing.

"I have often thought about the similarity of these different religions," Stendahl said, "in terms of losing the self being the key to finding the self. Your book emphasizes self-denial. The Buddha has intensified our understanding of faith as non-self-seeking."

Pfister and Freud

"This material in your book about Pfister and Freud is fascinating," Stendahl said. "I was particularly struck with this comment of Freud's, 'Most people don't care about the purpose of life. What they care about is being happy.'"[*****] Stendahl had circled this comment in

---

[*****] Freud said, in "Civilization and Its Discontents," *Standard Edition*, vol. 21, p. 75-76:

The question of the purpose of human life has been raised countless times . . . . Only religion can answer the question of the purpose of life. One can hardly be wrong in concluding that the idea of life having a purpose stands and falls with the religious system.

We will therefore turn to the less ambitious question of what men

red, making it more prominent than anything else in my book.

"When you are brought up in a bourgeois-Christian, *noblesse-oblige* society such as I was brought up in Sweden," Stendahl said, "you are taught not to expect to be happy. The lower classes might strive to be happy. But a sophisticated person would be looked down upon if their goal in life were to be happy. The goal of life is to serve God, and to take care of one's obligations to others. The word 'prestige' can be used only with a negative connotation in the Swedish language. If one is concerned with one's prestige, if one cares what other people think, that is considered a negative attitude. In the society I was brought up in, one is supposed to do what one thinks is right, and let the chips fall where they may, without caring whether other people like you or don't like you. That is how much the Lutheran church had an influence over the culture. Hypocrisy is the ultimate sin.

"But nowadays the culture is different," he continued. "Now the mental health movement has such a vast influence, especially in the United States, but also in Sweden. Now everyone is out to be happy. What is true and what is right counts for nothing. All that counts is whether the person is going to get re-elected.

"This is such a striking comment about Freud," Stendahl said, pointing to the red circle. "What is the context of this comment? Did Freud propose that happiness was a better value than was meaning? Did he propose happiness as an alternative to religion?"

---

themselves show by their behavior to be the purpose and intention of their lives. What do they demand of life and wish to achieve in it? The answer to this can hardly be in doubt. They strive after happiness; they want to become happy and to remain so. This endeavor has two sides, a positive and a negative aim. It aims, on the one hand, at an absence of pain and unpleasure, and, on the other, at the experiencing of strong feelings of pleasure. . . .

As we see, what decides the purpose of life is simply the program of the pleasure principle. . . . yet its program is at loggerheads with the whole world. . . . One feels inclined to say that the intention that man should be "happy" is not included in the plan of "Creation."

"No," I replied, "Freud didn't set up a horse race between happiness and meaning in life. He indicated that life would have meaning only if one had religion. I think he was a bit jealous of Pfister, because Pfister had a sense of meaning while Freud didn't."

Stendahl persisted. "Did Freud imply that happiness is better than meaning, is a higher value if the two are ranked?"

"No," I replied. "I don't think Freud was all that negative about religion. You have to remember that Pfister was his best friend, or one of his best friends. As Freud saw it, he simply didn't have the option of finding meaning in life because he started with atheistic assumptions."

"So that's why you think he had this subtle jealousy of Pfister," Stendahl said.

"Yes," I said, "but it is not overt. He never says that he is jealous that Pfister had something he wished he had."

"But this is such an amazing comment," Stendahl said, pointing again to the red circle he had drawn on my manuscript. "'People don't care about meaning. What most people care about is being happy.' It is a comment that describes everything we see around us today. When did Freud write this?"

"In 1929," I said. "I think this comment of Freud's was the beginning of the unravelling of our civilization."

"What did Freud mean by such a comment?" Stendahl sounded perplexed. "Did he explain himself, or was it just a side comment?"

"The comment has to be understood in the context of the essay *Civilization and Its Discontents*," I said. "Freud argues that humans are not naturally civilized. Our basic nature, which he calls the 'id,' is to pursue individual pleasure, such as by unbridled sexuality, orgies, blind aggression, etc. The nature of civilization is to subdue and curtail human nature. This is done through psychological methods. Inside each person is a superego which functions like an armed garrison stationed in a conquered city. The purpose of an armed garrison is to suppress uprisings, to assure political domination of the city, to extract taxes, and to keep the natives under control. Similarly, the superego inside each of us suppresses our instinctive desires, and that is why all of us are unhappy, in Freud's view. For this reason people are discontented with civilization. We are all at conflict with the civilized part of ourselves, but we yearn for liberty from this oppression so we could have more pleasure in life. But he didn't advocate that we rid ourselves of our superego and thereby become uncivilized."

Stendahl continued to listen attentively, as if he was trying to comprehend something remarkably different than his way of thinking.

"These ideas explain how psychoanalysis is conducted," I continued. "The analyst will say to the patient, 'Why don't you allow yourself to do X? You would enjoy X.' And perhaps the patient has a valid reason for avoiding X, such as saying that X would involve exploiting someone else. But the analyst might say, 'Well then, why don't you allow yourself to do Y since you would enjoy Y?' Perhaps the patient decides to get a little pleasure by allowing himself or herself to do Y. By this means the patient's superego becomes a little less tyrannical and less oppressive, so that the patient begins to enjoy life a bit."

"So this is a way of educating the superego," Stendahl said, "making it more sophisticated?"

"Exactly," I said. "Reducing the tyranny inside oneself, so that the superego is less like an oppressive police state."

It occurred to me that Stendahl didn't care much about whether he was psychologically oppressed. He cared about serving God, and as far as I could see, that was the absolutely dominant issue in his life. Yet at the same time, he seems to have enjoyed his life, especially his marriage. He and Brita obviously take delight in one another. His Nantucket cottage is a cute little house, the kind of place that a man wearing a hair shirt would not own.

"So this comment," Stendahl pointed a third time to his red circle, "was just a side comment of Freud's?"

"Perhaps you could say that," I replied. "But what Freud meant is not how these ideas are applied today. Today in the popular culture the idea is to throw your superego to the wind and pursue the pleasure of life. It is the whole basis of advertising, that if you buy this product you will be happy."

"It is the basis of everything today," Stendahl said. "When people shift their attention from serving God to psychological ideas, then even the quest for the purpose of life becomes a clinical tool: Let's give this person a sense of purpose so they will feel better. Of course, that is my whole complaint about the American way of conducting worship services. The attention is on the community, on the feelings of the people worshipping. The attention should be on God. One should worship God because God is God, not because it makes you feel good to do it, not because of what God has done for you. This whole attention today on the self is the wrong focus. God should be the focus. Then if one worshipped in an anonymous cathedral or in a local church it wouldn't matter, because the attention is where it should be."

I was struck with how Stendahl's mind turns to examples of worship services as easily as my mind turns to examples of patients I have treated. My line of work makes it natural to think of clinical vignettes to illustrate my ideas. His line of work makes it natural for him to think of worship services, and the use of the Bible in churches, to illustrate his ideas.

Soul Versus Self

"By the way," Stendahl asked, "how would you compare the words 'soul' and 'self'? Have you thought about that?"

"These two words are almost synonyms," I said. "When scholars translate the Bible, the word 'soul' is used in one translation, while 'me,' 'myself,' or 'I' are used in another translation.[94] So from a Bible translator's viewpoint these words are almost interchangeable."

"This gets back to what you said before," Stendahl said. "You don't **have** a soul, you **are** a soul."

"Yes," I replied. "But in the secular world the words 'self' and 'soul' are not synonyms at all. In the secular world 'self' refers to the whole person, without any reference to God. The discrepancy between 'soul' and 'self' is that one word implies a Godwardness, while the other word does not.

There is even a branch of the mental health movement called Self Psychology, created by Dr. Heinz Kohut. This is the major form of psychoanalysis today, the heir to the Freudian tradition. The emphasis in that school is on the entire person, called the 'self'."

"What is this fellow's name?" Stendahl asked.

"Kohut," I said. "Heinz Kohut." Stendahl wrote it down.[95]

"So Kohut has a holistic view?" Stendahl asked.

"Yes," I replied, "it is holistic in the sense that Kohut emphasized the person as a whole, without subdividing the person into conscious versus unconscious parts. Yet it is not holistic from my vantage point. Did I ever tell you Boyd's teaching on this subject?"

Stendahl began to take notes, which was a surprising shift in our relationship, after all the years I had sat at his feet taking notes. "What is the Boyd teaching?" he asked, sounding amused.

"Boyd teaches that there are three aspects of the self which are missing from the mental health perspective," I said. "First, God's relationship with the self is omitted. Second, the self's future after death is omitted. And finally the invitation to begin today to live by the values of the Kingdom of God is not mentioned by mental health therapists. For these three reasons the mental health experts do not treat the whole person, but only part of the person. Thus if we refer to the whole person as a 'soul,' then for the sake of clarity, it would be best to say that the 'self' is only the secular aspect of that soul."

Stendahl nodded.

"That's good, those three points," he said. "I like that. It seems that somehow today the 'self' has become too important. There is too much emphasis on it. That is because our culture is so thoroughly psychological."

"Our culture is psychological because the Christian church no longer talks about the soul," I replied, "and therefore the mental health movement has moved in to try to fill the vacuum. Remember when I last saw you, in November at the Society of Biblical Literature annual meeting in San Francisco? I had asked twenty-five Bible experts whether 'psychiatrists and psychologists today treat what in biblical times would have been called the "soul?"' Fifteen of them said yes, compared to four who said no. The remainder couldn't decide."

"And do you remember what I said at that time?" Stendahl asked.

"You said the numbers weren't important. You said I should pay attention to the reasons that were stated to support those answers."

"That's right," he said. "Anyway, what troubles me is that the self has become too important. The mental health movement seems to encourage that."

"I agree," I said. "I think of the mental health viewpoint as being pre-Copernican. Prior to Copernicus the sun was thought to revolve around the earth. In the mental health way of thinking everything revolves around the self. If they talk about God at all, which is rare, it is that God revolves around the self, enhancing the self, making the self stronger and more cohesive, or else inducing guilt feelings in the self. That entire psychology is erroneous, Boyd says."

Stendahl was still taking notes. I was feeling in my glory, giving my mini-lecture to my aging mentor and guru.

"Boyd says that the post-Copernican worldview is that the self is in orbit around God. This means that we should forget ourselves and attend to God as the focus and gravitational center of our lives," I explained.

"I absolutely agree," Stendahl said. "It is what you quote me as saying in Chapter 10, that the word 'soul' suggests a Godwardness. That is a psychological orientation that is different than what is implied by the mental health word 'self.' It is different than what is going on today in popular culture. I think there is even a magazine called *Self* sold at the checkout counters of grocery stores."

"Yes," I said, "I think you are right. But this pre-Copernican viewpoint is found in every magazine sold at the checkout counters of grocery stores."

"Yes," he said. "That is because the whole world has become psychological. Now about the second of your three points, you talk about the self having a future after death. I am often puzzled about the continuity."

"The continuity of our identity," I asked, "between now and Heaven?"

"Yes," he said. "The dust of our bodies disintegrates, but something survives. Have you thought about what survives?"

"I'll tell you one thing for sure," I replied. "It is clear to me that at a minimum there will be continuity of memory. I say there must be continuity of memory, because we will be judged, and therefore we will have to be able to remember our deeds here on this earth. It is not possible to imagine that we will have Alzheimer's in Heaven, that we will be unable to remember what we did and said here on earth, for otherwise it would not be fair for God to judge us."

"I like that," Stendahl said. "'Continuity of memory.'"

"You know the mental health movement thinks of time so differently than I think of time," I said. "Psychotherapists focus on the present moment, and they focus on the past. In order to free you up to enjoy the present moment, they go back to analyze your past."

"All the way back into the womb," Stendahl said.

"So in psychotherapy a client is often 'working through' their past," I continued. "But I have never heard a single example of psychotherapy 'working through' the exciting future which lies ahead of us: after death. To me, and I think to you, that is the decisive time frame, what lies ahead. My whole life is shaped by anticipation of what lies ahead, yet that issue is ignored in psychotherapy. Of course, when I say it is exciting, I am speaking of Heaven, and ignoring the first fact, which is that we must be judged."

"Judged." Stendahl lit up like he had something important to say. "Yes, but judgment is such a tricky issue, because the word has been used to stir up such guilt feelings, especially by the evangelicals. You want to be careful when talking about judgment. You want to make sure your audience doesn't understand you as condemning them, making them feel guilty. I have four Bible passages that I love to quote about judgment."

Stendahl got out his *New Oxford Annotated Bible* again, with its red cover. It is so strange talking with this man who repeatedly breaks off the conversation mid-sentence to go hunt up the exact verse in the Bible. He seems to have memorized most of it. I say this because he has often practiced what he calls "biblical arithmetic" with me. This means that one person says something like, "Ecclesiastes 12:7 and Genesis 2:7 are the mirror images of one another." The other person knows immediately what is meant, because both have not only memorized the Bible, but the verse numbers as well. I might know that piece of biblical arithmetic, but mostly I feel ignorant when he cites verse numbers and I can't instantly call them to mind.

"Aha," Stendahl broke out of his reverie. "Here it is:

> For God will bring every deed into judgment, including every secret thing, whether good or evil (NRSV: Ecclesiastes 12:14).

"I always think that is marvelous," Stendahl continued, "that we are going to be judged by a God who knows every secret thing, who sees us with complete clarity, who knows us completely. It is such a profound idea. We can know that God will not judge us based on superficialities, but based on a thorough understanding of everything about us."

He sounded as if he were lost in sublime thought, ready to meet this Judge. So deep was Stendahl's rapture after he read that verse that I was reluctant to upset the apple cart with my next comment:

"Today I think many people look to their psychotherapists for that sort of complete knowledge," I said. I probably wouldn't have introduced such a rude thought if Stendahl hadn't earlier told me that in Sweden a person is supposed to simply state the truth and allow the chips to fall where they may. "Today people share themselves honestly with their therapist, and look to the therapist to know 'every secret thing, whether good or evil.' When someone is going through a dark night of the soul they don't think of turning to God in prayer, nor do they think of God as their judge.

They think of 'seeking help.' And this strange word, 'help,' means getting into psychotherapy."

"Yes, I know that." Stendahl sounded slightly annoyed. I wasn't sure whether he was annoyed at the stupidity of modern culture, or at me for breaking his rapture. It was clear to me that Stendahl does not face his final Judge with overwhelming feelings of guilt and worthlessness.

"And that is how I understand Psalm 139 also," Stendahl persisted. Once this man is locked in on his target, like a cruise missile, nothing will deflect him. He had told me there were four Bible verses about judgment, so I guessed he was now onto the second of those.

"You know Psalm 139, eh?" he asked, looking me in the eye.

I felt like I might flunk the arithmetic test again. "Uh, well, uh, well . . . ." Searching my memory, I was trying to find the index card for Psalm 139.

"'O Lord, thou hast searched me and known me, Thou knowest when I sit down and when I rise up,'" Stendahl let me off the hook. "Now this isn't meant in a threatening way. It does not mean, 'You had better watch out, because God is monitoring every detail of your behavior.' No! It means that God has this clarity of vision, that God knows us through and through. This implies a judgment that is fair, not one that is superficial. Isn't it marvelous, the clarity . . . ."

Again his voice lapsed into a sense of reverie.

This time I listened quietly, waiting to see where he was leading me this time. This man has led me on more wild adventures in my life than Indiana Jones. Once, years ago, Stendahl told me that the Bible says that God speaks to us through dreams and visions. That comment alone cost me a decade, as I went to the Carl Jung Institute in Zürich, then spent ten years making notebooks of my dreams, trying to figure out if the Bible was right or wrong. No, I am not going to answer that question here. My point is that I have learned, after Stendahl has sent me off on one quest after another, to listen attentively when he falls into a state of ecstasy and meditates on the Bible. As I sat patiently, eventually Stendahl came out of his apparent trance and said:

"And then there is 1 John 4." Suddenly Stendahl sounded perplexed. "John 4," he was leafing through his Bible again. "God knows everything . . . ." He was turning pages back and forth, searching, scanning, ". . . knows everything . . . ." "I could find that verse in a second if I had my computer," I said.

"Yes," Stendahl replied, "but you would have to have at least a few words right." Stendahl doesn't use computers, but admires those who do. Still he was searching. "Aha," he said, "the problem is it is earlier than I thought. It isn't in 1 John 4 but 3. It says we:

will reassure our hearts before him whenever our hearts condemn us; for God is greater than our hearts, and he knows everything (NRSV: 1 John 3:19-20).

"So," Stendahl sounded triumphant, "it doesn't say that God will condemn us even worse than our superego. This is not a heavy superego type of judgment. It is a judgment by a God who knows everything, who is greater than our hearts."

I may be no good at biblical arithmetic, but I am able to count to four. It seemed clear that Stendahl had cited only three Bible verses about judgment. Again he had begun to look absorbed in sublime thoughts about God judging him in the not-distant future. I waited quietly as a gentle drizzle fell on the shrubbery around his Nantucket cottage. His sister had died two days earlier. It was clear to me that death was much on his mind. It was her meeting with God and his own which, I imagined, must be absorbing him. I felt lucky that he had allowed me to come to his house, given the circumstances. He would not talk to me much about his grief about this sister he loved so deeply. But he lapsed into these silences lasting several minutes, apparently contemplating God's judgment of his family. Suddenly he broke the silence and spoke.

"And then there is Psalm 103, eh?" Stendahl peered at me.

This time I knew for certain that I would flunk the arithmetic test. He was leafing through his Bible again, intent on finding the precise wording.

"'As a father pities his children,'" Stendahl read, "'so the Lord pities those who fear him. For he knows our frame; he remembers that we are dust' (NOAB: Psalm 103:13-14). ****** So God knows that we are dust, meaning that God knows our weakness, our frailty, and will take that into account when judging us. He knows our frame." He laid great emphasis on the word "frame."

Stendahl's frame looked more rickety than when I first met him a quarter of a century ago. I was flooded with so many memories and feelings about him because I was preparing myself to say goodbye. During this interview, which was so poignant, Stendahl was probably saying goodbye to his sister, and I was saying goodbye to a man who has had more influence over my life than any other.

"The Lord knows us and pities us," Stendahl continued. "God takes into consideration our frailty, and knows we are made of dust. God knows our frame. There is no shame in our frailty. So those are the four biblical verses I quote at funerals, when people want to know about judgment.

"Imagine to be judged by One who knows us really, fully. Imagine a judgment where justice and mercy are rolled into one . . . ."

****** The *New Oxford Annotated Bible* (NOAB) is based on the old *Revised Standard Version.* The NRSV is slightly different:

As a father has compassion for his children, so the LORD has compassion for those who fear him. For he knows how we were made; he remembers that we are dust (NRSV: Psalm 103:13-14).

In whose hand is the **soul** of every living thing, and the breath of all mankind.

(KJV: Job 12:10)

In his hand is the **life** of every living thing and the breath of every human being.

(NRSV: Job 12:10)

Thus might we procure great evil against our **souls**.

(KJV: Jeremiah 26:19)

But we are about to bring great disaster on **ourselves**.

(NRSV: Jeremiah 26:19)

Conclusion

... that are hated of David's **soul** ....

(KJV: 2 Samuel 5:8)

... those whom David hates ....

(NRSV: 2 Samuel 5:8)

Chapter 19
The Relationship of
Religion and Mental Health

The soul emerges as intensely private. Many of the people I have interviewed about the soul told me that they had never discussed with anyone the issues about which I was asking them — not even with their psychotherapists or their spouses. Religious folk are loathe to cast their pearls before those they don't trust (Matthew 7:6). Only because of my credentials did they judge me trustworthy. My priesthood made me trustworthy vis-a-vis discussions of God. My psychiatric credentials made me trustworthy vis-a-vis mental health issues.

In each chapter of this book, the religious and psychological themes are knit together into one fabric. Each person weaves them together into a unique culture. They cannot be separated without unraveling who the person is. As someone named Chuck Sheppard once said to me, "Mental health and religion are like two rails of a railroad track. They are parallel and never meet in the external world. But the journey of the soul cannot be made without both rails."

In the inner and private world, mental health and religion comprise a common culture. That inseparable culture is called "the soul." The way one person internalizes religion is unique to her psychological makeup, and is different than the way another person takes religion into her soul. The differences are not due to denomination or to theology, but to differences in the mental health culture inside that person.

Judeo-Christian Religion
and Mental Health

One of the many paradoxes of this book is that the secular world views mental health and religion as quite different. How do I conceptualize the relationship between these two approaches to the soul?

In the Bible our faith is spoken of as "the way" or "the path." In Greek the word for "the way" (Greek: 'odos or hodos) might also be translated "the road."[96] The Hebrew Bible was written before the Romans built roads. The corresponding Hebrew word was "the trodden path" (Hebrew: derek) and is most vividly illustrated by the First Psalm.[97] One of the shared goals of mental health and the Judeo-Christian tradition is that both seek to help people who feel lost and directionless. The difference is simply one of emphasis.

Mental health focuses on the potholes in the road and tries to help people who are stuck in the mud by looking to see why they are stuck. Psychotherapists are experts when the road has been washed out by a flood, or obliterated by a snowstorm. Mental health professionals do not deal with the direction of the road. Nor do they always address the question whether it is the right road or the wrong road, or a road going nowhere.

Our faith focuses more on the direction of the road. The faithful are referred to as "seekers" who have a general sense of their goal, even if they have not yet reached their destination.[98]

It is important to faith that one makes a commitment. Even if they have not reached the destination, the faithful are committed to going in that direction.

People get stuck for various reasons. My experience is that insoluble psychiatric or emotional problems often have religious answers. Insoluble religious questions often have emotional and psychological answers. Remember what Paul said when he indicated why he was in need of some psychotherapy: "I do not understand my own actions. For I do not do what I want, but I do the very thing I hate" (NRSV: Romans 7:15).

"How should I live my life?" is a religious question. It is not a question that psychotherapists can answer. Not even psychoanalysts claim to provide an answer. If one stays in psychotherapy long enough, certain religious questions eventually arise. For example:

a. Why do I live?
b. To what or whom do I devote my life?
c. I yearn for something greater than myself, but what?
d. What is the purpose or meaning of my life, given that I am to die?
e. How can I endure suffering?
f. How do I stop being so preoccupied with myself and my problems?
g. What is the larger significance of my life?

Psychotherapists have no answers to these questions. Biological psychiatry certainly doesn't claim to provide answers to questions of this magnitude. But every religion provides rich and interesting answers.

He seeing this before spake of the resurrection of Christ, that his **soul** was not left in hell, neither his flesh did see corruption.

(KJV: Acts 2:31)

Forseeing this, David spoke of the resurrection of the Messiah, saying, "**He** was not abandoned to Hades, nor did his flesh experience corruption."

(NRSV: Acts 2:31)

Appendices

And we were in all in the ship two hundred threescore and sixteen **souls**.

(KJV: Acts 27:37)

We were in all two hundred seventy-six **persons** in the ship.

(NRSV: Acts 27:37)

Appendix A
The Illusion of a Future
A Friendly Discussion with Prof. Dr. Sigmund Freud
By Oskar Pfister
Pastor in Zürich

Translated by Ted Crump and Jeffrey H. Boyd, M.D.

[Translator's Note: This essay by Oskar Pfister, *Die Illusion einer Zukunft: Eine freundschaftliche Auseinandersetzung mit Prof. Dr. Sigm. Freud*, was published in 1928 (*Imago* 1928; 14(2/3): 149-184) and has never before been published in English in its entirety.][99]

Dear Professor!

In the kind manner that is your custom during our nineteen years of collaboration, you asked that I publish my objections to your booklet *The Future of an Illusion*. You have generously made available one of the journals that you publish. Thank you for this new evidence of your friendship.

Your unbelief you have long made clear to me and the entire world. The fact that you now prophesy a religionless future is no surprise. I, on the other hand, see in the psychoanalytic method that you have created a splendid means of purifying and promoting religion. You will laugh as you did during the time of the famine when we plodded along Beethoven's footpaths in snowstorms through the heights of Vienna. For years we have been unable to convince each other on this point. In every other respect I have been willing to sit at your feet, inundated with richness and blessings from your abundant intellect.

Your book was for you an inner necessity, an act of sincerity and a courageous expression of your convictions. Your titanic life work would have been impossible without the shattering of idols, whether they stood in universities or the vestibules of churches. You serve science with a reverence and ardor that elevates your study to a temple — this is known to everyone who has had the pleasure of coming close to you.

As I told you before, I am suspicious that you struggle against religion because of your own religion. Schiller warmly extends a brotherly hand to you; will you strike it away?

I do not concur with the clamor of individual guardians of Zion. Whoever has fought so enormously as you have for the truth and strives so heroically as you have for the liberation of love, is a true servant of God, whether he wants to hear it or not. That is the Protestant yardstick for measuring a true servant of God. He is not far from God's Kingdom who creates psychoanalysis as an instrument by means of which **suffering souls** cut through their fetters, and prison gates are opened so that they can hasten into the sunshine. Jesus tells a fine parable of two sons, of whom one dutifully promises to go to his father's vineyard, but does not keep his word. The other stubbornly rejects his father's unreasonable demand, but nevertheless fulfills it (Matthew 21:5,28ff). You know how cordially the founder of the Christian religion prefers the latter son. Are you angry that I see you literally nearer the throne of God than many churchmen who mumble prayers and whose hearts have never glowed from knowledge and good will toward men? I see you catching such marvelous rays of the eternal light because you have been consumed in striving for truth and the love of mankind, despite your alleged unbelief. I envy you, because the Gospels teach that everything depends on God's will, and does not depend on who says "Lord! Lord!"

And still I decisively oppose your judgment of religion. I do it with the modesty that befits the humble, but also with the joy with which one defends a holy and beloved matter.

I feel the earnestness of truth that your strict school has fostered. But I also do it in the hope that many who have been frightened away from psychoanalysis by your rejection of religious belief will again befriend it as a method and accept its empirical insights.

I do not wish to write against you, but on your behalf. For whoever enters the lists for psychoanalysis battles for you. I battle on your side as well. You and I are concerned with nothing else than to overcome illusion through truth. Whether you with your *Future of an Illusion* or I with my "Illusion of a Future" will come closer to the ideal will be decided by a higher tribunal. Neither of us wraps ourselves in the prophet's mantle; rather we are content with the modest role of a meteorologist, but meteorologists can also make mistakes.

Yours very cordially,
Oskar Pfister

I
Freud's Critique of Religion

1) The Charges

In his booklet *The Future of an Illusion*, Freud makes religion out to be an illusion. This is a different concept of illusion from that which usually occurs. As usual, it includes the trait of error and invalidity. But Freud emphasizes: "An illusion is not necessarily an error"; "we call a belief an illusion if in its motivation wish fulfillment comes to the forefront. We thereby disregard its relation to truth, just as illusion itself dispenses with its authentications." In another connection in his treatment of the truth-value of religious teachings, Freud declines to take a position.

Accordingly, one could reckon with the possibility that religion still will be accorded validity. Freud's example of the illusion of Columbus, that he had found a new sea route to India shows this. For even if the discoverer of America did not reach India, nevertheless others did on the route that he opened. The Genoese also reminds us that thinking that is predominantly realistic can be invested in illusion. Without the observation of the curved surface of the sea and the implication that the earth is round, the brave journey toward the west would not have been undertaken. I call attention now to the inner amalgamation of wishful and realistic thinking: The question is whether religion is like a very large part of knowledge in general, such that it is possible to segregate illusion from realistic thinking. Or does realistic thinking struggle in vain to scrape out concreteness beyond wishful thinking? But wait! I do not wish to tell tales out of school and do not wish to tie myself down — see what follows!

The hope that Freud had left religion an altar to whose horns it can flee does not hold up for long. For we soon learn that religion is comparable to a childhood neurosis. We learn that the psychologist is optimistic enough to assume that the neurotic phase will be overcome. Admittedly it is not certainly overcome, but the hope is clearly expressed. More precisely, the neurosis which religion represents is described as "the general human obsessional neurosis." Obsessional neurosis derives from the relationship with the father, as does the Oedipus complex. To this Freud adds the prognosis: "According to this concept, one could foresee that the turning away from religion must come about with the fateful inexorability of a growth process, and that we find ourselves right now in the middle of this developmental phase."

The apex of the complaint is found in the sentence: "If, on the one hand, religion brings with it obsessional restrictions exactly as an individual obsessional neurosis does, on the other hand it comprises a system of wishful illusions together with a disavowal of reality, such as we find in an isolated form nowhere but in amentia, a state of blissful hallucinatory confusion."

Finally, religion is recognized as a protection of civilization. However, religion fails in this respect, especially because people do not achieve the desirable happiness and moral restraint through it either.

Let us examine these charges more closely!

2) Religion as an Obsessional Neurosis?

We begin with an examination of the nature of the obsessional neurosis that religion is supposed to bear. Unquestionably, Freud is completely correct in this respect. The psychology of religion is indebted to him for this discovery, inasmuch as many expressions of religious life are burdened with it.

These obsessions are unmistakable in many primitive religions which know nothing of church, as in all the orthodoxies. We also know that this great misfortune of religions was inherited and imposed in the cradle. It comes from the effect of repressions of instincts as demanded by the bioethical progress of mankind.

It is the tiresome fate of our species that the simple and the expedient for the most part are found only on the detour through monstrous eccentricities. The history of languages and moral views shows this as clearly as the development of religion.

But if this obsessional burden is difficult to deny even in the first stage of religion, the question still arises whether it is essential to its nature. Could not this collective neurotic tug be harmless, or even work to the advantage of the whole? Is the obsessional burden of religion like the tail of a tadpole that is better off lost?

Religion involves renunciations of instinct gratifications. However, is this not the case in all civilizations? Anyone who primarily exhausts himself no longer has the requisite energy for cultural achievements. If we imagine a purely instinctual existence, then we imagine that it belongs to animals, but is not part of human nature. A purely instinctual existence is almost always denied by the wise frugality of nature. In humans we find an Ash Wednesday protest, but not a purely instinctual existence. The concept of nature is comprehended one-sidedly and quite inadequately if one understands it "naturalistically." Vegetating animals are not a better model for human nature than is civilization. In fact, the nature that surrounds us makes mental ascent a necessity. Civilization is always the product of two natures: outer and inner human nature. Civilization itself is not contrary to human nature, it is a development of human nature. The necessities that entice civilization, and the renunciations that it entails, arise out of our human nature. If the concept of nature is freed of its false constriction, this same mutual harmony of man and the surrounding world is perceived as a cultural development. This demonstrates for us a theory of knowledge for the process of knowing.

I do not accept the statement that the formation of religion was based on the renunciation of egoistic drives, while a precondition for neurosis is the repression of exclusively sexual drives. Specifically, the history of the Oedipal relationship shows that sexuality makes up an integrating component of the egoistic drives and vice versa. The singling out of individual drives can be undertaken only as an abstraction. As soon as one believes that the drives (apart from their most primitive impulses) are really separate, one falls into error after error. This "organic viewpoint," as I call the correct way of looking at things, is indispensable for comprehension of the genesis of religion. I do not believe that Freud and I disagree in this regard. Since he now describes the negative father fixation as the main determinant of religion, he also allows the libidinous forces to be recognized. I believe that one should search in a very wide area for the drive denials that lead to religion. The pathways that go into the formation of religion also exhibit an extraordinary multifacetedness. The totem cult is based on entirely different determinant complexes than, say, the socioethical monotheism of the classic prophets of Israel. The aesthetic and pacifistic cult of Aton are entirely different ones from the Spanish conquistadores. But drive denials that are more or less comprehensive and cause deep repressions must naturally have an effect on every religious formation.

Is the formation of obsessions always inherent to religion? I believe, on the contrary, the highest religious formations specifically abolish obsession. Think, for example, of genuine Christianity! Jesus opposes his "command" of love against the obsessive-compulsive legalism. He says the legalists impose a heavy yoke by means of their scriptural literalism and painstaking ceremonialism. "You know that it was said to your forefathers — but I say it unto you" (Matthew 5) — here we have the powerful act of redemption. And it does not take place by virtue of a new obligation. Rather it takes place based on the strength of the authority of the freedom that was won by dint of victorious love and recognition of the truth. Jesus overcame the collective neurosis of his people in accord with a good psychoanalytic principle when he introduced love into the center of life. It was, of course, a morally perfect love.

In Jesus' idea of "father," which is completely purified of the dross of the Oedipal tie, we see all the heteronomy and awkwardness of the enthrallment entirely overcome. What is expected of man is nothing else than what corresponds to his essence and his true destiny. What is expected of man also fosters the common good and promotes maximal health for both individuals and society. This clears a place for the biological point of view. It is a terrible misunderstanding to understand Jesus' main commandment — "Thou shalt love God with thy whole heart and thy neighbor as thyself!" (Matthew 22:37ff.) — as a law in the Mosaic spirit. The form of the imperative is retained, but it is an obvious irony that love can be carried out only freely. Thus the commandment loses the character of a law.

How finely Jesus practices psychoanalysis 1900 years before Freud!

Admittedly, one should not understand the expression too strictly. I have spoken about this elsewhere (*Analytical Spiritual Welfare*, Göttingen, 1927:20-4). I recall that Jesus does not simply suggest the symptom away for the cripple, but rather enters into the underlying moral-religious conflict, mediates it and thus overcomes the paralysis from within. His belief in demons may alienate us as metaphysics, but as neurology we acknowledge it. The psychological approach from which Jesus challenges the biblicistic coercive authority would be completely approved by the modern analyst (e.g., Matthew 19:8: The Mosaic law on the divorce certificate is allowed because of the hardness of men's hearts).

Jesus' treatment of the transference, which is assumed to be love, deserves the admiration of all pupils of Freud. The transference is led further to achievement of absolute ideals, so that no new obligation comes about. Jesus abolishes the obsession-producing fixation on parents by asking his followers to dedicate themselves to the absolute father, who is love.

Not that one may describe Jesus as the first psychoanalyst in the sense of Freud, as cheeky little whippersnappers might perhaps like to do! But his redemptive **cure of souls** points so decisively in the direction of psychoanalysis that Christians should be ashamed to have left to a non-Christian the exploitation of these illuminating footprints. Undoubtedly, the reason lies in the fact that the obsessive-compulsive neurotic bungle of religion threatens the structures of religion and all structures of the human spirit. This obsessive-compulsive neurosis submerged these wonderful footprints. Similarly, early psychiatry was submerged in materialism.

We could trace Jesus' elimination of compulsion and weakening of its determinants still further. We could demonstrate how his idea of "father," in contrast to Oedipal hate, is free of all reaction formations. Jesus said that God does not want sacrifices, but rather should be loved in one's brother. We might recall that brotherly love in its deepest and broadest sense is the characteristic feature and star of Christian doctrine. We might recall that the goal and highest good of all striving and yearning lie not in personal satisfaction, but rather in the Kingdom of God. The Kingdom of God is the rule of love, truth, and justice for the individual as well as for the universal community. However, we would be distracted too far.

And cannot something quite similar be said of Amenhotep's religion, in a certain sense even of Buddha's? Protestantism contains a powerful redeeming principle, namely freedom of belief and conscience. There is also its requirement for love. This involves not only a liberation from religious compulsion, but also a general healing of all forms of compulsion.

It is very unfortunate that Freud leaves out of consideration precisely the highest expressions of religion. Developmentally, it does not occur that religion creates compulsions and holds man fast in neurosis. Rather the pre-religious life creates neurotic compulsions, which then leads to the corresponding religious concepts and rites. The magic that precedes religion is not yet religion.

The Judeo-Christian religion is the greatest religious development. Fanned by a higher, ethical, and sociobiologic insight, a religious inspiration (revelation) repeatedly comes to the surface and endeavors to remove compulsion and create freedom. However, new shackles are repeatedly forged, as no one understands better than the analyst. Then a later religious concept must arise to break those shackles. It is obvious that this religious struggle for redemption corresponds to a humanization process.

Thus pre-Israelite animism and naturism, Judaism, Baalism, classic prophetism, post-exile legalism (reaching its culmination in pharisaism), birth of Christianity, Catholicism,

Reformation, Old-Protestant orthodoxy, pietism, and the Enlightenment follow one after the other. The present-day offshoots of the various Christian compulsion and compulsion-opposing systems likewise follow after one another. However, we should be mindful of the fact that at the present time compulsion-free individualism is very strongly represented within Protestantism. This has been recognized for its social pathos on the one hand and its strict critical-scientific work on the other. Religion must not put aside any independent development whatsoever! If the Christians at one time or another rivaled the wildest barbarians in acts of cruelty, this did not occur as a result of rigorous exercise of their religious principles. It happened by dint of neurotic illnesses which distorted and ravaged the Christian religion. Similarly, drives and artistic creation were subjected to and took on the most abominable distortions.

Accordingly, I flatly deny that an obsessional neurosis is intrinsic to religion as such.

3) Religion as a Creation of Wish-Fulfillment

Freud does not claim to be the first person to state that religions represent only wish-fulfillment creations. Almost ninety years ago Feuerbach (L. Feuerbach, *The Essence of Christianity*, Quenzel, Reclam:40) elaborated the thesis of theology as disguised anthropology and of religion as a dream. However, Freud refined and fortified these assumptions on many points with the use of his **soul microscope**.

One should not delude himself on this. Wishful thinking is an element in religious formation. The mere explanation of the latent wishes, working to make them more evident, and exposure of the Oedipal situation make it entirely impossible to deny this.

But is all religious thought explained by this? And is this muddling of wishes and realistic thinking the special property of religion? Or should in religion and science, indeed even in art and morals, the repression of wishful thinking by realistic thinking and the mobilization of realistic thinking by wishful thinking comprise the ideal towards which mental development strives — gasping, hoping, and repeatedly and painfully disappointed?

Before we turn to the examination, let us look around from a common starting point. I will never forget that bright Sunday morning in the spring of 1909 in Belvedere Park in Vienna when Prof. Freud in his kindly, fatherly manner pointed out to me the hazards of the research he was carrying out. Even then I declared myself ready to lay down the priest's office so dear to me if the truth required it. To proclaim a faith that is refuted by reason seemed to me a juggling trick that I wanted nothing to do with. Nor did I want to turn my head toward the abode of unbelief, but in my heart to stick to belief. I did not know what I would have to change if I followed Freud. One does not stake his soul on illusions.

I have moved towards Freud's position a good distance (Feuerbach also met the approval of theologians for his psychological critique of religious teachings). I have always been aware that the concepts of God and the hereafter are often painted with colors from the palette of wishful thinking. I found traces of the father, or of different pastors, in a hallucinated image of God. Behind that, I found the rule of hate. It was a clear connection. But I didn't perceive anything tremendously new or unexpected about this.

I had long known that wishes mirror their originator in the whale-rich hereafter of the Eskimo, in the green happy hunting ground of the Indian inviting him to collect scalps, in the mead-flowing, tournament-favoring Valhalla of the Teutons. It is similarly the case in the prayer room heaven of the pietist or in Goethe's hereafter with its moral showdown.

Nemesis would have it that even the God-deniers whom I analyzed were extraordinarily often guided by wishful thinking. What analyst has not found atheists whose unbelief turned out to be disguised father rejection? However, it is erroneous to press all rejection of religion into the wish scheme.

Let us look more closely at the wishes that lead to religion! It is a given that initially they are largely of an egoistic nature. Is this any different in science? Could one expect a disinterested thirst for knowledge from a primitive? Even in the so-called child of nature we see how necessity reigns in cult and belief, e.g., the necessity for atonement of injustices committed (e.g., the death wish against the father). With moral development the religion also matures. Selfish wishes recede more and more, even if there are recurring relapses into egoistic thinking. This is a sign that the wild and primitive are not easily rooted out.

The classic prophets of ancient Israel dispensed with personal continuance after death. All their hopes and endeavors were in their people.

In the Gospel we see instinctual wishes powerfully fought against. Jesus' development advances in constant battle with tradition. We see ideas of reward, race, and sensuously colored conceptions of the hereafter repressed. The ideas of reward are far more clever and wiser from a psychoanalytic standpoint than in the categorical imperative. The categorical imperative imposes a rigorous, emptying philosophy with its lack of understanding for love. What Jesus demands in the name of his religion is directly opposed to egoism. Nevertheless, Jesus with great wisdom never proscribes self-love. Jesus' religion is directly opposed to masochism, as it was practiced by the ascetics. Jesus advocates gentleness and humility, self-denial and rejection of the accumulation of riches, and dedication of one's own life for the sake of the greatest moral good. In short, the entire life style demanded of his disciples by the Crucified of Golgotha is diametrically opposed to the pleasures of primitive human nature.

However, it corresponds to a higher concept of human nature. This higher human nature could not have arisen from the lower instinctual demands. This higher human nature could arise only from a realism. This realism was won under harsh necessity and originated from a grandiose intuitive anthropology and cosmology. In the Lord's Prayer all that is egoistic disappears — the request for daily bread, this minimum of subsistence, is no longer egoistical, the universal ethical ideals govern, and topmost stands the bending to God's will ("Thy will be done!"). This is no Buddhist contentment, but it is also no pathogenic introversion. The assertion is false that according to Chistian belief, everything that earthly life denies will be made up for in the afterlife. It is Islam but not Christianity that teaches that relinquishment of sexual activity is made up for in the hereafter. Jesus emphatically states that sensuous expectations from life are to be ruled out after death (Matthew 22:30).

His highest ideal, the Kingdom of God, has the earth as an arena. The content of the Kingdom of God is the ideal of ethical and religious wealth, which have nothing to do with instinctual wishes.

An opponent might object: Don't wishes of a higher order arise from religion? I counter: One must understand the difference between wish and hypothesis. A wish ends in the hallucination of manifestations of satisfaction. A wish does not trouble itself with the actual circumstances. Thus we know many religious phenomena which make this illusory leap from desire to assumption of an existence. However, no one will assert that every wish comes to be satisfied in such an illegitimate manner. One can find satisfaction of his wishes very realistically.

Jesus felt the imperative of love in himself, which contradicted the sacred tradition.

We can still see the stage in which Jesus believed he could reconcile the claims of inner requirements with those of the Mosaic law (Matthew 5:17-22). However, this view was not pervasive (Verse 27ff., 33ff., 38ff.). An open break with the Mosaic law was inevitable.

The inner necessity in Jesus had to overthrow the outer Mosaic law. This inner moral necessity itself must have originated from God. And because it ended in love, God had to appear as a loving God, no longer as the strict, jealous God of the Old Testament. Therewith, as was shown above, the fear-inspiring compulsive character of the Torah broke down.

Jesus acted out of intuition.

If we wish to translate it into cumbersome acts of cognition, then we make it into a hypothesis. This does not say: I wish this and that, therefore it is real. Rather it says: This and that exists; what must I regard as real in order that this particular existing thing becomes comprehensible? The hypothesis proceeds from something existing, and concludes another existing thing, which results from the first by logical necessity.

Natural science with its hypotheses follows a similar path. The difference is that here we are dealing with existentials, from which one advances to other existentials. In the hypothesis, on the other hand, the starting point is made up of an assessment or an imperative. Kant, for example, regards the categorical "Thou shalt!" as the Archimedean point and postulates a lawgiver from this.

I myself proceeded from another ethical certainty: the stipulation to love one's neighbor, oneself, and the absolute ideal. This was thrust upon me by both psychoanalytic and sociologic considerations. From this norm I had to conclude that there is an Absolute as the origin of all values.

This way of thinking is a peculiarity of being human; in its Is lies an Ought. This philosophical operation is nothing else than Jesus' intuitive certainty of God, based on empirical evidence. A multitude of wishes of one's own taste must be sacrificed. Even many "needs" of firm knowledge of reality must be sacrificed. The stipulation to love is really logical, if its basis is itself applied as intellectual and loving.

Furthermore, the question arises: Doesn't science also contain in disguised form symbolic fantasy? Does not scientific thinking also work with anthropomorphisms, which both reveal and conceal much? I still recall the happy astonishment with which I read Robitsek's significant study of the scientific accomplishments of the chemist Kekulé of Stradowitz in the first volume of *Imago*. According to this, the structure of benzene and theories about benzene originated from visual fantasies of dancing partners and snakes. But the alert intellect must test these dreams.

We realistic thinkers of the Twentieth Century must take care not to regard all primitive concepts which strike us as fantastic as being the products of wishful thinking. If the savage suspects boiling water to conceal a live animal, what wish would guide him? The idea suggests itself to him because he is familiar with the water movement caused by a hiding animal, but is unfamiliar with boiling water, and therefore thinks by analogy.

It is not just religion which projects human-like forces and beings into natural manifestations and processes! We find arguments by analogy even in the proudest halls of natural science. We find it even in the strict discipline of philosophical thinking. We speak of "force," "cause," "effect," "law," and a hundred other concepts, which long ago were found by epistemology to be anthropomorphisms. Is not the concept "censor" of the same nature?

The history of the sciences is an ongoing struggle with anthropomorphism and other disallowed projections of known facts into the unknown. Why should religion and theology be an exception?

Has theology, which has taken up religion, got one foot stuck in the stage of wishes? If this was the case, then I would seriously fear (or should I hope?) that this is a pitiful loss of scientific method. But it is a pitiful loss of scientific method that is shared with the other sciences: natural sciences and history not excluded. Philosophy has this problem. Philosophy may come to be sanctioned as pure objectivity, and added to the natural sciences. They lack that which they seek: pure experience, from which the additions of human subjectivity are weeded out. Instead, the natural scientific contemplation ends in the bitter insight that it discerns only a tiny spot on the surface. This is admittedly still only a glowing pretense.

From the viewpoint of science, the colors vanish into "harmonies in the ether." One adds resignedly that the ether may be a very doubtful concept. Sounds turn out to be oscillations of the air. When sounds combine into a melody or symphony, the natural sciences have no place for that.

The atom has been conceived over several thousands of years as an absolutely simple and unchanging lump of reality. The atom, which was at the center of the scientific worldview, is found one morning to have broken up like a piece of coal and transformed into other elements.

Natural law is revealed to be a product of wishful thinking. The wish is that under the same circumstances a process must always come about in the same manner. After all, think of the confusion of engineers and bridge builders if it behaved otherwise! If the natural sciences have yielded something certain, it is the insight that in their realms we remain stuck up to our necks in wishes. Pragmatism is often dismissed with a wrinkled nose. However, pragmatism still has the quality that it unveiled the interest of the practical American in an extensive construction of reality. There is a wish behind all cognition.

Theology has abundantly proved itself to be able to relinquish wishful thinking. However, I believe that I can demonstrate this more expediently at the conclusion of our friendly discussion. Along with theology, religion also was subjected to the most profound sacrifices; it sacrificed most painfully for the sake of wishing.

From the very beginning, religion has been able to incorporate into itself knowledge of nature and values. Whoever mocks Joshua's standstill of the sun should take into account that the concept of a firmly established and unified natural order still did not exist at that time. A unified concept of the natural order appeared in science over two-and-a-half millennia after Joshua. Recently, this concept of a unified natural order again lost considerable credit. Christianity struggled for a long time, far too long, against Copernicus and the theory of evolution, but finally came to terms with them. Christianity should not be blamed for not following all the scientific fads of the day. A number of prominent natural scientists right up to the present day find no difficulty in reconciling religion and natural science. The people who proclaim the incompatibility of the two are usually the half-educated people at a table in the tavern. However, such people make their proclamations with much greater ease than great researchers of Freud's rank.

Having said all this, nothing is proven as to the truth or untruth of religion.

But what about the contradictions of religious thinking? I have already spoken about the sincere efforts of the newer theology to overcome them. It is difficult to decide whether this has been successful.

I believe that I have arrived at a religiousness that has mastered the contradictions. I have mastered the contradictions, despite the fact that unsolved riddles have remained at every turn, as in every other area of human thought.

But now I will turn the tables and ask: Isn't empirical science bursting with contradictions the size of your fist? I will not mention crippled concepts such as the ether. Ether is alleged to be a substance that does not consist of atoms! Nevertheless, ether was greeted by honest natural scientists with the most subservient bows, as if ether was a prince. Significant natural scientists and psychologists, such as Herbart and Wundt, assign to philosophy no other task than to eliminate contradictions and reconcile the cleared-up empirical concepts with each other. Here one certainly should be somewhat more forbearing with the religion of the uneducated and of the theologist.

Freud did not intend to enter into the individual contradictions and limited himself to declaring most religious teachings as unprovable and irrefutable. Therefore, I cannot enter into a defense of the reality of religious ideas. Natural science has learned to humbly restrict itself to the realm of the provable. Recognizing this modesty of the natural sciences, we should be cautious not to demand of other disciplines that which we ourselves cannot provide. With what exemplary restraint Freud speaks of the provability of his statements! We must be very mindful not to take agreement of what has been learned for clarification and validity of a doctrine. It is very often only a sign of fatigue, and the feet of the gravedigger perhaps are already standing in front of the door.

In this situation, wherein our truly scientific active seems dubious compared to the passive, we must guard against the danger of cheating. As a result of wishful thinking and admission of contradictions, one would not arrive at a more favorable balance.

However, one can also see no reason to put all his assets in the one bank of science and give up all other cultural goods as superfluous. More on this later.

When Freud reproaches religion as hallucinatory confusion, he undoubtedly is correct about some forms of religion. However, does this apply to all forms of piety? I don't see that. Again the great master appears to hold very definite forms before his eyes and to generalize. I almost believe that he was an infrequent guest in a Protestant worship service. Freud was seldom exposed to serious theological discussions. We analysts know that something very large and deep can lie behind hallucinatory confusion.

When Paul attests that his preaching of the crucifixion to the Gentiles is foolishness (1 Corinthians 1:23), this is no counterargument to Paul.

To me, a creative Dionysian or Appolonian fireball who does not give out his revelations as clarified wine, but rather as fermenting must, is much more valuable than a sober scholar who expends his life force in sterile word-juggling and pedantic preciseness. The degree of sensibleness is not necessarily the measure of value. Stormy youth, then, with their mad acts and foolishness, have a considerable advantage over the reason of old men. One cannot wait to eat and drink until the physiologists have completed their diet analyses and have developed their nutrition theories to everyone's satisfaction. Radium baths served well for a couple of centuries before radium, and therewith the origin of the curative success was discovered. Is it unthinkable that in the mental area knowledge of causes, panting laboriously, lags behind the possession of worthwhile goods? Protestantism with its incredibly strict and sharp criticism has retained too little rather than too much of the Platonic fury and Paulinist scandal. And still I cannot do otherwise for my part than to follow the reality principle with relentless strictness. I am constantly concerned that valuable good will be lost from the meshes of scientific ideas.

Although one may reject scientific hypotheses, one cannot reject the practical questions on whose resolution the structuring of life depends. One must take a position on such practical questions, even if stringent proofs are lacking. How otherwise should one establish a family, take up a profession, etc.? Thus in our religion there lies a trust. Woe to him who marries, chooses a profession, and assumes a religion only according to his wishes without taking a careful account of reality!

4) Religion as Anti-Intellectual

Is religion intrinsically anti-intellectual? Freud writes: "When we ask on what their claim to be believed is founded, we are met with three answers, which harmonize remarkably badly with one another. Firstly, these teachings deserve to be believed because they were already believed by our primal ancestors; secondly, we possess proofs which have been handed down to us from those same primeval times; and thirdly, it is forbidden to raise the question of their authentication at all."

Granted that such horrible argumentations have surfaced here and there. But what educated Christian today would let himself be frustrated with such answers? Certainly not we Protestants. We criticize the Bible and dogmas just as radically as Homer or Aristotle. As regards the Catholics, at least they preface their dogmatism with an apology which attempts to satisfy the demands of reason. As a philosopher, one can contest its logical necessity. As a pupil of Freud, we can diagnose the Catholic apology as a rationalization. As a Protestant, we reject at least a part of it as a *lettre de cachet*, but there still remains a mental effort which commands respect.

The Protestant religion arises out of thought, and therefore we Protestants allow thought its full latitude. Even if Luther did not grant reason the rights it deserved, still he was a theologian and a scientific thinker, otherwise he would have never become a reformer. Zwingli went through the humanistic school, which added not only the leniency, but also the clarity of his theology and piety. Even the grimmer Calvin, Geneva's sinister Grand Inquisitor, availed himself of his juridical thought in his fortress-like theology. The religion of the reformers was also the result of their scientifically schooled professorial thinking. The newer theology has strictly realistic thinking. This theology has and still achieves much with its radical negation, and intends to render the most appropriate service to religion by realism. No one has ever forbidden me to ponder over religious matters. On the contrary, we Protestant pastors require free critical thinking from our pupils. In ministers of free orientation, this is well understood. It is even true of many conservatives. We calm frightened persons who have fallen into crises of faith with the assurance that God loves the sincere doubter. We teach that a faith solidified by thinking is worth much more than faith simply accepted and learned. We also require and support free thinking in the religion of adults.

According to Freud, thinking should be weakened by religion. Admittedly, he immediately adds that perhaps the effect of the religious prohibition against thinking is not as bad as he assumes. But nevertheless he regards it worth the effort to attempt an upbringing free of the sweet poison of religion.

A long chain of the most profound and freest spirits, who have enormously enriched the intellectual life of mankind, have simultaneously endorsed both religion and science, religion often with the greater intensity. I cannot believe, as Freud assumes, that they would have accomplished even greater things if they had never heard anything about religion. I will single out a few names from the long list: physicians such as Hermann Lotze, Wundt, Kocher, physicists such as Descartes, Newton, Faraday, Robert Mayer, chemists such as Justus Liebig, biologists such as Oswald Heer, Darwin, Pasteur, K. E. von Bär, mathematicians such as Leibnitz, Pascal, Gauss, geographers such as Ritter, historians such as Johannes von Müller, Carlyle, Niebuhr, L. von Ranke, statesmen such as Lincoln, Gladstone, Bismarck, philosophers such as Kant, Fichte, Schelling, Hegel, Herbart, Ruskin, Eucken, Bergson, poets such as Goethe, Schiller, Rückert, Bitzius, Gottfried Keller, K. F. Meyer, Geibel.

These people betray no intelligence defects, although they believe in God. There is no reason to think that their minds would have soared up to even greater things if they had not encountered religion. Some of the persons certainly stand far above the average of the believers in religious intensity. One would have expected the opposite if the danger of intellectual stultification was so closely linked to religion.

Even recent natural scientists like Einstein, Becher, and Driesch found their thinking leading them to believe in a will that created the world. But we do not base the proof of the truth of religion on these authorities.

Freud placed importance on the fact that the drive to think in children would be impaired if one said "God made them" when people asked the question as to the origin of natural objects. I agree with him. But I would like to ask whether the result is any different if one says that nature made them? In religious teaching it is always pointed out that God works through natural events and through human action.

My own thinking was richly fertilized by religion. One cannot stick his head in the sand with regard to life. Religion suggested to me many rational problems, and presented me with magnificent historic figures. Religion inspired my sense for greatness and moral necessity. I would find it an intolerably great loss if the religious recollections were torn from my life. Even the fact that when I was a child the Bible was presented to me as the infallible word of God sharpened my thinking. I still remember how as a twelve-year-old, after a lecture on the story of the flood I ran to the Zoologic Museum in order to compare the measurements of the ark with those of the glass cabinets. On this basis, I created a childish theory of evolution. At the same time, I adopted a skeptical attitude toward the Bible. This skeptical attitude was later transformed into free criticism.

Freud proposes irreligious instruction of children. This has already been done. It has been massively applied in communist circles for many years. In my analyses, I often had to deal with persons who were reared without religion. I cannot confirm that it led to an increase in intelligence. It did not lead to a more advantageous development of the predisposition to think. Atheistic philosophers are not intellectually superior in my opinion: Consider Karl Vogt or Moleschott or Häckel. Thus far history has judged otherwise.

5) Religion as a Protector of Civilization

Let us examine religion as a protector of civilization. Here Freud expects a police mission. "Religion has clearly performed great services for human civilization, contributed much towards taming of the asocial instincts, but not enough. If it had succeeded in making the majority of mankind happy, in comforting them, in reconciling them to life and in making them into bearers of civilization, then it would have occurred to no one to strive for a change of existing conditions. But what do we see instead? That a shockingly large number of people are dissatisfied with civilization and unhappy in it, that they feel it as a yoke which must be shaken off; and that these people either apply all their strength toward changing this civilization or go so far in their enmity to it that they will have nothing at all to do with civilization and restriction of instinct."

I agree completely with Freud that religion sometimes has proved itself to do a poor job as policeman of civilization. But I would like to add that it seems to me lucky that things are this way. Religion has more important things to do than to protect the mix of nobility and loathsomeness that is called civilization!

By civilization Freud understands "all that wherein human life has risen above its animalistic conditions and wherein it differs from the life of an animal." He rejects a separation of culture and civilization. "Civilization encompasses on the one hand all the knowledge and capacity that men have acquired in order to control the forces of nature and extract its wealth for the satisfaction of human needs, and, on the other hand, all the institutions necessary to adjust the relations of men to one another and especially the distribution of the available wealth."

In my view, there is an enormous amount that is disgraceful and harmful among those things which elevate man over the animals. Cruelty, injustice, and poisonous seeds permeate our knowledge and capacity to satisfy human needs, the institutions for regulation of social relationships and distribution of wealth. Religion should not attempt to retain the existing state of affairs. War, the spirit of Mammon, hedonism, mass misery, exploitation, suppression, and countless other injuries point to the necessity to differentiate between good and bad. The good is worthy of protection, and the bad must be combated, in what is today called civilization. I think that Christianity, if taken seriously, must strive for very profound and radical changes in our superficial and stunted civilization. Religion should become a leader and beacon out of our apparent civilization to true civilization. Religion should not be a preserving police force!

It is unworthy of religion if one assigns it the task of providing consolation for the instinctual renunciations demanded by civilization. It is unworthy of religion if one assigns it the task of providing muzzles or handcuffs for the asocial masses. This is the role that Freud sees for religion. The subduing of animal instincts (insofar as they impair human welfare and human dignity) is the other side of the coin of the positive goals. Religion should unleash the highest mental and emotional forces, stimulate the highest achievements in art and science, fill the life of all people, even the poorest, with the maximal wealth of truth, beauty, and love, help to overcome real life necessities, build new forms of social life that are truer and richer in content, and thus bring to life a higher, innerly richer humanity, corresponding better to the true requirements of human nature and ethics than our much-extolled uncivilization.

Nietzsche has called our uncivilization the thin skin of an apple over a glowing chaos. One completely fails to recognize the essence of Christianity if he believes that it offers him heaven as a substitute for the misery that the world has afforded him. The prayer "Thy kingdom come!" imposes the obligation to apply all our energies toward building an earthly kingdom of God. This is similar to the commands of the

Gospel, which are also very much of this world. The Sermon on the Mount demands: "Leave there thy gift before the altar, and go thy way; first be reconciled to thy brother, and then come and offer thy gift" (Matthew 5:24). Jesus cannot help it if Christianity misunderstands this so often. Freud provided us with the capacity to see why the intentions of Jesus Christ have so often been disfigured into a caricature by an obsessive-compulsive distortion.

There is no truer realism than Christianity. Reality consists not only of what can be seen or perceived by the olfactory organs and other **windows of the soul**. Reality consists also of that which lies behind the windows in the base of the **soul**. Reality consists also of what lies behind the sources of our **soul's** excitement. It requires a somewhat deeper penetrating view of the essential nature of things in order to see this. Realism is impoverished if one neglects these higher realities lying on the other side of visible and solid objects. We will postpone this problem for a moment.

II
Freud's Scientism

1) The Belief in Science
Bringing Happiness to Mankind

Freud counters religious belief with the belief in the power of science to bring happiness, by which Freud understands only empirical science. In it the illusion of truth has given way. Here he is faced with the question: What is science? Apparently this is less of a concern than Pilate's question: What is truth? Freud is a positivist, and we can thank God for that. Without his concentrated dedication to the empirical, he would not have become the great pioneer. Freud fails to notice that at the same time that he attempts to strangle religious illusion, he heralds another illusion — belief in science as the Messiah!

But first let's allow the master to have his say! Freud is much too precise a thinker to blindly put his trust in vulgar uncritical belief in the omnipotence of the natural sciences. He does not shrink back from the question "whether our conviction that we can learn something of external reality through the use of observation and thinking in scientific work" has a sufficient foundation. Like a true philosopher, he continues: "Nothing should keep us from directing observation toward our own selves and from applying thought to sanction its own criticism. Here a number of differentiations open up, whose result could not but be decisive for the construction of a *Weltanschauung*. We surmise, moreover, that such an effort would not be wasted and that it would at least in part justify our suspicion." "But such a comprehensive task is beyond the capacity of this author, and of necessity he will narrow his study to pursuing only one of these illusions, namely that of religion."

Later, however, empirical science is elevated to a bold perspective with an optimistic future. After abandoning religion, man will expand his powers with the aid of science. Man will then learn to tolerate the great necessities of fate with humility.

Freud immediately concedes that perhaps this hope is also of an illusory nature. What? Then perhaps we need only exchange religious illusion for scientific illusion? The difference would be that religion fools us for sure, and science fools us perhaps? We would therefore remain in a state of uncertainty, and the last word would belong to skepticism. Skepticism is at least sure of one thing: that doubt has its full logical justification.

Still, Freud shows that religion is not the only source of consolation. Like a knight, he raises his lance for the intellect: "The voice of the intellect is quiet, but it does not rest until it has been heard. In the end, after countlessly repeated rejections, this still comes about. This is one of the few points about which one may be optimistic about the future of mankind, but in itself it is not of little importance. One can attach still other hopes to it. The primacy of the intellect certainly lies in the farther, farther, but probably not in the endless, distance. And since it intentionally sets itself the same goals whose accomplishment you expect from God — in the human scale, naturally, insofar as the external reality, the *Anagche* [Greek], allows it: love of humanity and reduction of suffering, we dare say that our opposition is only temporary, and is not irreconcilable. We hope for the same thing, but you are more impatient and — why should I not say it? — more egoistic than I or my people. You want to let bliss begin immediately after death . . ." "We believe that it is possible for scientific work to learn something about the reality of the world, by which means we will increase our powers and in accord with which we will be able to direct our lives. If this belief is an illusion, then we are in the same position as you, but science with numerous and significant successes has proved that this is no illusion." "It will continue to develop and be refined. However, it would be an illusion to believe that what science cannot give us we can get elsewhere."

With this magnificently logical statement, Freud concludes his prophecy of the demise of religion and the glorious autocratic rule of science. The god of Logos knocks the god of religion from the throne and reigns in the Kingdom of Necessity. We have not the slightest knowledge what this Kingdom of Necessity is.

2) Historical Illumination

This scientific ideal has a venerable history. Freud refined it by his positivism and strict scientific attitude. His empiricism is completely different from that of the English empiricists. The English empiricists seized the world of experience with precision, but left guidance of actions to natural instinct and the conscience. John Stuart Mill, with his absolutely irreligious upbringing, finally sought support from religion.

The Future of an Illusion also departs completely from the positivism of an Auguste Comte, who first smashes the mythologic, then the metaphysical stage of thought in order to sing the praises of the sciences, which alone are capable of bringing bliss. Comte then tries to explain the world from the moral feeling of man and constructs a highly romantic and fantastic religion based on man. This indicates that Comte's scientism, resting on a wide base, is not enough for him.

David Frederick Strauss proposed a mechanistic materialism rather close to Freud's thinking. Strauss takes an excursion into philosophy which Freud would not share, by assuming a "reasonable and good universe." Strauss calls for an ethic which cannot find satisfaction in science. Of all the philosophers I know, the Baron von Holbach comes closest to Freud. He derives the creation of the idea of God from the wish to make the forces of nature accessible by humanization of influences on them through prayer and sacrifice. Von Holbach contests the usefulness of religion. For that reason, he seeks to put an end to it. He poses lasting happiness as the goal of striving. It is self-evident that Freud towers over this materialist of the Eighteenth Century as an empiricist and dispenses with his banal metaphysics.

3) Freud's Scientific Optimism

Now we are faced with the task of examining Freud's scientific optimism. First we must clearly understand what he understands by science and how far his optimism goes. We have no more precise information about the first point. Freud has been decisively negative toward philosophy. I learn to my satisfaction that Freud grants fundamental legitimacy to the theory of knowledge: He says he will provide an answer to the question whether we can learn anything of external reality. Freud, in fact, decisively evades the task. He explains that science must limit itself to presentation of the world as it must appear as a result of the peculiarity of our organization. He says that the problem of the nature of the world must be an empty abstraction without consideration of our **soul's** perceiving apparatus.

Here Freud would have delivered epistemological results without a preceding theory of knowledge. He assumes as self-evident that we are dealing only with a world of appearances. Does not the essence of science consist of just dissolving this world of appearances and counterposing abstractions to it, which gives us our first understanding of this world of the senses? As we have already heard, optics breaks down colors into oscillations of colorless "bodies," which are again robbed of their "corporeality" by physics and chemistry, and are reduced to energy, electrons, and other incorporeal abstractions. We nowhere see and smell causality, we point to it in appearances.

The "soul's perceiving apparatus," which, according to Freud, all investigation of the nature of the world should take into consideration, is by no means a clear structure protected from deception. Can I measure temperature with a thermometer without being certain of the reliability of the instrument? Can one ignore the entire history of modern philosophy? Descartes dealt with absolute skepticism. In Hume the illusion of certain causality was smashed. In Kant the illusion of empirical knowledge was overturned. And in the most recent natural science a true twilight of the gods was evoked. One falls into a scientific labyrinth if one thoughtlessly incorporates epistemological and metaphysical concepts under the deceptive heading of natural science. Has it been forgotten how natural science arose with its concept of natural law, the atom, air, Laplace's world formula, etc.?

There is no natural science without metaphysics. There never has been and never will be.

I myself passed through the school of empirical criticism and for a couple of semesters sought a "pure experience" in the sense of a recognition of reality that would be completely free of all subjective ingredients. An idle enterprise! The world is accessible to us only through our **soul's** organization, and not through the gate of the senses. Our senses guarantee no knowledge at all. Our categories of thought, whether one thinks of them in Kant's sense or otherwise, always play a part. Therefore, we must practice critique of knowledge. Moreover, we need concepts such as cause and effect, even though they are anthropomorphisms. We need atoms and molecules, etc. Whoever shies from abstractions must keep his hands off science. Even measuring and weighing deal with abstractions: for numerical concepts are, like all concepts, abstract. Whoever does not earnestly grapple with philosophical problems talks about empiricism with an amateurish confusion.

Moreover, how can one deal with the religious problem if he does not take the basic questions of epistemology into consideration? It is simply a negative dogmatism to proclaim that the world will and world mind do not exist.[100]

If one believes that philosophy is a crazy notion in the heads of people who are far removed from life and reality, then let us point out that the history of philosophy features a number of brilliant names of men who have made enormous contributions in physics, mathematics, astronomy, etc. When a contemporary, acclaimed natural scientist of the rank of a Driesch turns to philosophy, then it should be noted that philosophy does not just deal with quirks and brain twisters, but with a reality whose existence cannot be brushed aside with a wave of the hand. The same is true when psychiatrists turn to philosophy.

In my view the world of spiritual order, which can be inferred from the world of appearances, stands more certainly before us than the certainly deceptive world of sense perception. For certain one can make it easy on himself and confess to agnosticism. But this declaration of the bankruptcy of thought is not made so easily.

Freud has a popular concept of science. I do not know how far scientific knowledge reaches, what degree of reliability it can acquire, and what chances are granted to it. Therefore, how should I know whether or not there is a spiritual first cause and an ordering, that is, a thinking world will? How can I know whether the spread of power through knowledge will bring added happiness to man?

Let us examine Freud's prognosis for science. One cannot say that he gives us a rosy-fingered Aurora. Freud is much too serious and honest a man to make promises that he is not convinced he can keep. Man with the aid of science will expand his power, how far we do not find out, and will learn to bear the great necessities of fate with humility. This is all, entirely all.

But has not Freud said too much even with this? Civilization could soon collapse. The demise of the western world is prophesied to us by a man whose abundant knowledge is universally recognized. Is it possible that a civilization guided by science will overcome the wild passions? The world war has revealed to us the barbarism that lurks in the depths of people. Eduard von Hartmann and many others guarantee to us that the growth of the sciences will only increase our misery. It has been agreed with such certainty that the progress of the sciences has so far increased the total sum of human joy in living. But even if this has been the case thus far, there is no certainty that it will be true in the future. Is it certain that we are happier than we were one hundred years ago? This may be the case for educated people. But are the workers more satisfied, thanks to the blessings of science, than a few generations ago? Or the craftsmen? Or the farmers? The wonderful achievements of technology are not much use if they are pressed into the service of human avarice, human cruelty, and inhuman hedonism.

Freud's prognosis for science is based on a simple argument by analogy that I do not regard as confirmed. It runs as follows: Because thus far the progress of science has brought advantages to mankind, this will be so in the future as well.

Or, better expressed, there is in the background a belief in science, whose basis Nietzsche spotted with his eagle eye and put to words: "It will be understood . . . that there is always a metaphysical faith, on which our faith in science rests, that we the intellectuals of today, we the godless and antimetaphysicians, also still take our light from the fire that a faith thousands of years old ignited, that Christian faith which was also the faith of Plato, that God is truth, that the truth is divine . . . But how, when this becomes ever more unbelievable . . . ?"

Do we know from an oracle's pronouncement that knowledge will always contribute to the increase of human happiness, even if evil passions are the decisive factor? Byron complains: "The tree of knowledge is not the tree of life!" Can exact knowledge refute him? And if a Faustian thirst for knowledge burns in us, can natural history and medicine (philosophy and theology are disqualified) satisfy us today, or does the heart also purely burn for the Faust of today?

Freud foresees that man will learn to tolerate the necessities of fate with humility. Many people have been able to do this without science from time immemorial. If I also bow before the **greatness of soul** of the irreligious who preach this humility, who will tell me that humility in particular must be the last word and why? Some individuals have shot a bullet through their head in despair, although they stood on the proud battlements of science. Others were carried away in wild hatred of life and strove to drug themselves with dissipations. Others became introverted in anti-worldly mysticism, etc.

Perhaps a wish is hidden behind Freud's belief in the final victory of the intellect. His prophecy of the end of an illusion includes the deployment of a new, specifically scientific illusion. The fact that the deployment in Freud does not take place with drums beating and flags waving, but rather very subdued and with tentative steps, is in accord with his humility. But I cannot join in, specifically because the reality principle is standing in the way in a warning manner.

4) Freud's Belief in the Sufficiency of Science

"It would be an illusion to believe that what it [science] cannot give us we can get elsewhere." Freud's confession of faith culminates in these words.

The context makes it clear that he has knowledge of the world in mind. He is also thinking of a substitute for that which religion offers its believers.

I follow Freud with joy and fascination on the wonderful paths of his empirical science. However, at this point it is impossible for me to keep pace with him. Here Freud's radiant intellect becomes intellectualism, which, intoxicated by its successes, forgets its boundaries.

We humans are not only thinking apparatuses, we are living, feeling, desiring beings. We need possessions and values. We must have something that will satisfy our dispositions, enliven our will. Even thinking must offer us values. In analysis we are often dealing with people who don't think clearly, people whose thinking is almost starving and in despair. We carry within us a conscience which directs or rewards us. Psychoanalysis has specifically demonstrated the power of guilt feelings. Freud shows more clearly than anyone in the world the decisive importance of judging, of feelings, affects, and drives. As we know, the intellect does not know how to judge. The sharpest mind cannot tell whether a symphony of Mahler or a painting by Hodler is beautiful. The cleverest person can without inner contradiction hail a cruel betrayal and mock a heroic death in the service of truth. A heartless cad can have a clear-seeing intelligence, and a mental weakling can be indignant over a perfidy. Science lacks the ability to judge aesthetic and ethical values. Indeed, it seems that one can still hear Aristotle's definition of the brain as a cooling apparatus. Thinking is characterized or extolled as an emotion-subduing function, as Spinoza pointed out.

It is obvious that Freud must accommodate the emotional values somewhere in his scientific scheme, since his own life manifests such a wonderful abundance of emotional values. But I do not find the place in his concept of science.

I also do not see where he places the temple of art. Would art really be a sign only of something unanalyzed and weak? Could science replace for us the loss of the Beethoven symphonies or Reger sonatas? And the wonderful works of Egyptian, Hellenic, and Christian art: we should sacrifice them for scientific theorems and findings? The marvelous cathedrals that comprise the pride and joy of our race, the paintings drawn from Christian feeling of a Fra Angelico, Leonardo da Vinci, Albrecht Dürer, Holbein, down to Gebhardt, Thoma, Steinhausen, the "Pieta" of a Michelangelo, "The Thief" or "The Lost Son" of a Meunier,[101] etc., this should all disappear? The fountain of Christian poetry, as it sends out its silver waves in Lessing's Nathan, Goethe's Faust, Dostoevskii's Idiot, Tolstoy's Resurrection, etc., would have to run dry.

Instead of these green meadows of art, only the moor of theory would remain, on which the ghosts of error would flutter around menacingly. Would the glorious future of science in the coming millennia be stubbornly reserved for the skeptic, who never once could sigh with Faust: "O, happy is he who can still hope to rise up from this sea of error!"?

To me, art still reveals the deep secrets seen by the messenger blessed with prophetic eyes. It is a priceless treasure revealed. Art reveals things which have escaped and will escape the glasses of the scholar. Art is a miracle for feeding **hungry souls**, a message of peace from the realm of ideals. It is something which no philosopher's fist can ever tear down, because it belongs more certainly to the true reality than to the blatancies and other pretenses of the mind. To work this out intellectually, I would need a longer discussion. In this discussion the intellect would be given only the role of the explainer to whom the creative genius pays homage and serves.

O, how I would dread a scholarly state emptied of art!

And even less can inventive science replace for us the realm of moral values and forces. Science must incorporate itself into moral goal-setting, if it is not to sink into doubtful enterprises. Who would contest that in Freud it belongs to an ethical plan and helps him carry it out? But in his booklet, if I see things correctly, no place is reserved for this comprehensive consideration. We no longer agree with Socrates that knowledge itself is power. The alcoholic, who knows that he is destroying himself with his vice, still does not have the strength to break with it. Also the analytic insight into the dynamics of the unconscious and its deepest roots still does not help one to become free of its spell. Freud teaches us that through transference the shut-in instincts must likewise be released.

Is it really settled that with increasing science the cast of men's minds will be purified? Alexander von Öttingen showed that there is a higher percentage of criminals among the highly educated people than among the intellectual middle. Academicians have unbelievably petty views. When almost one hundred years ago the public school was created, a rapid decline in criminality was expected. And today?

Why do we have the certainty that in the future the growth of science and technology will also conjure up a rise in moral forces? In the fight against alcoholism, I have clearly experienced how little can be achieved with scientific arguments. Science may overcome the repressions, but the towline of science cannot achieve that morality which lends worth and true inner health to life.

That is why I do not believe in the replacement of religion by science. Religion is the sun which has brought forth the most magnificent flowering of art and the richest harvest of moral ethos. All the very great, colossal art is a prayer and sacrifice before God's throne. Philosophers of religion speak of God as being the basis for the ideal. However, for the pious, God is the basis of his realistic creation, the Pentecostal spirit, which descends to earth in tongues of flame, the revealer, whose "Let there be light!" also illuminates the darkness of men's souls with a blinding clarity. Whoever would destroy religion would cut through the taproots of the great art which reveals the deepest meaning and the highest powers of life.

And likewise we see in religion a supporting pillar of morality. Moral insight has been incorporated into pious faith. This continues to be true, as the history of Christianity teaches us. The boldest and most marvelous ethical advances could take place only as religion. We do not have the scientists to thank, but rather the religious writers, for the great progress in ethics. Even Kant is basically only the learned spokesman of Protestantism turned toward Puritanism. And Kant signifies a serious relapse behind the ethics of Jesus, because Kant rules out love.

It has not been noted that ethics itself is marching forward. I cannot agree with Freud's thesis that the moral is always self-understood. As we know, one cannot simply rely on conscience. In moral science the most diverse doctrines wave their hands at each other in agitation. Flat utilitarian morality seems an abomination to the Kantian. Eudemonism with its enigmatic unclarities irritates the Nietzschean, who desires and canonizes the will to power as the measurement for good and evil. In these ethical problems, we see a chaos of contradicting concepts. One might think, for example, about the moral judgment of the war, excess capital accumulation, free love, abortion, etc. The positivist thinking, science, as Freud seems to have it in mind, can certainly not bring us any further. Even if it provides the most valuable building blocks for ethics, which will forever remain a philosophical discipline, and, in addition to sociology, above all Freud's psychoanalysis. Most recently in a public discussion, I heard the Viennese jurist Kelsen explain how positivism never has been able to create legislation (Kelsen himself is a positivist!). How then should positivism be able to bring about a system of theories? Empirical science lets us down in the formation of ethical concepts. And what is more important? The creation of a moral life has never been achieved with dry theories and clever concepts. It would be schoolmastery of the worst sort to fail to recognize this.

Religion can provide ethics. Religion provides partly elevated, partly loving symbols, with its poetic magnificence and its shattering interpretations of reality. Religion gives us thrilling personalities, who with their heart-winning deeds and sufferings draw one under their spell, and with their faults and weaknesses in part warn us away. These personalities give the fallen person courage to strive after his ideal with new strength.

Religion comes with an enormous metaphysical background and perspectives on the future. Religion divinely sanctions the moral commandment. Religion offers a message of redemption. This message of redemption anticipates some of the most important achievements of psychoanalysis. This is accomplished by means of a higher obligation and an alliance with the ideal world, which requires us to to overcome all resistance of the empirical world. This is certainly the expression of a higher reality. It is a reality which can easily take up in itself all the gifts of science. But it adds to these gifts an unheard-of abundance of other riches. Religion is a teacher of the materials and forces of life. Science with its theories is certainly not able to replace religion. But, even if the belief were untrue, we would still have to fight against it despite its accomplishments. Better to go to hell with the truth than to heaven at the price of lying!

Freud in his tolerance praises religion as a protection against neuroses. Earlier he declared that since the weakening of religion, neuroses have increased extraordinarily. Perhaps Freud carries chivalry a bit too far? I see in the crowds of devout persons an enormous number of hysterical personalities and obsessive-compulsive neurotics. Apart from the fact that all orthodoxies are to be regarded as collective obsessional neuroses, we find in devout Christians a great number of psychoneurotics. It depends very much on the nature of the devoutness itself, how far it is carried. However, it is unmistakably true that the free air of the genuine Gospel creates an indispensable protection against the danger of neurosis.

This, however, does not exhaustively describe the range of religion. Religion cannot be reduced to enthusiasm for art, morality, and protection against neuroses. It is much more: Religion takes up questions of the meaning and worth of life. Religion encompases the desire for unity of reason according to a universal worldview spanning Is and Ought. Religion involves longing for a homeland and peace, and the urge for a mystic union with the absolute. Religion involves the soul shackling of guilt and the thirst for freedom and grace. It involves the need for a love that is transported away from the unbearable uncertainty of the earthly. The earth is a place where countless requests choke and worry the soul in a state of unfulfillment. Religion provides the equilibrium that lifts up the life of man to radiant mountaintops with indescribably pleasing vistas of afar. It fortifies the heart and elevates the value of existence by imposition of very heavy moral obligations in the spirit of love.

The irreligious cannot feel this, as little as can the unmusical have an inkling of the content of a musical poem by Brahms. Religion is not so aristocratic as art and the higher sciences. It is itself a stream in which lambs swim and elephants can drown. But the fact of the matter is, as the New Testament says: "Faith is not every man's thing" (2 Thessalonians 3:3). However, by faith we understand not only a concept, but rather a grasping of the entire inner man.

How poor science appears to us compared to this abundance. Here we could indicate only a very small part. There is not space for greater detail. Besides, words cannot express that which is inexpressible. It is no wonder to me that many of the most important scientists regarded their work as service to God and many of the greatest artists and poets have humbly laid their laurel wreaths before the altar of God.

Conclusion

What then should we think of the future of the illusion about which Freud complains? If it is an illusion, then I agree that it must fall and disappear. However, Freud did not wish to pose the question of truth at all; he emphatically emphasizes that the illusion could be true.

Therefore, I am of the opinion that realistic thinking must push forward as far as the essence of reality will permit. How this might come about I have outlined in the brief indications found in my work *Worldview and Psychoanalysis*. I indicated how a metaphysics would emerge from empirical science as a necessary logical supplement. I also indicated that from moral affirmation conclusions about the world mind and world will would be possible, even necessary.

A clarified religion can emerge only from a harmonic link between belief and knowledge, from a mutual penetration of wishful and realistic thinking. In this merger of wishful and realistic thinking, the realistic thinking must not experience any falsification of the facts.

However, does not the intrinsic content of religion sink into the abyss in this synthesis? Freud assumes so. However, I cannot share his assumption. In my view the substance of Christianity is not attacked in any way when we reject miracles in the sense of God's intervention in the natural course of things. For hundreds of years, millions of Christians have done this, and nevertheless saw in religion their most sacred treasure.

The God of modern theology, revised by philosophy and free of crude anthropomorphisms, is the world will. This world will ends in the realization of love in the highest moral sense. This world will is more exalted than the God who in the cool of the evening promenades and personally closes the doors of the ark. This world will is also more exalted than the God who uses the earth as a footstool. The allegorical speech of piety should contain no regression into inferior wishful thinking.

We no longer allow moral instructions to be dictated to us from holy documents. Rather we derive our moral instructions from the essence of man and the human community, as autonomous children of God.

We piously subject the ethical insight of previous times to testing and reserve every right of objection and rejection. These moral instructions are as holy to us as the rules of one religious document or another. The Bible has not become smaller, but rather more magnificent. This is because we are no longer suspicious of it as a paper Pope and infallible oracle, as the legal basis of courts of inquisition. Rather the Bible is subject to the most relentless critique, because of our evangelical freedom.

We have long rejected reward and punishment as dangerous means of education.

Moral precepts contain a hygiene which shares information about dangers threatening individual and social health. These moral precepts refer to a legitimacy which is decisive for happiness, misfortune, and the structuring of lives. The moral world order is for us not a present state, but rather a normative state. It is a concept and legitimacy whose tendency we can recognize from observation of the reality of life.

We attempt to express this in moral precepts which we ethically formulate as an expression of the highest cosmic striving for development. We recognize these moral precepts as willed by God and holy as a result of a dependence on the will of the Creator.

Thus morality in no way rests on a heteronomous authority, but rather on the autonomy of the individual and society. But morality does not rest on the coincidental discretion of individuals, but rather on their nature. And human nature in turn refers back to the last conceivable absolute authority. Can we dispense with this religious engrossment? Will the advance of the exact sciences make it superfluous? The present-day march to the right in the direction of orthodoxies should not be of importance for our judgment. From the nature of man and the narrow limitations of the intellect, I must oppose Freud's prophecy of the future of an illusion. His *Future of an Illusion* is no longer prophetic, but rather a psychologically based assertion of the illusion of such a future.

To me, it is very gratifying that Freud himself basically strives after the same goals as I: he with his brilliant scientist's view, I with my limited means. He "intentionally" pushes his God Logos, by which he understands the intellect, toward the goal of love of mankind and reduction of suffering. For me, my God Logos is based on the first chapter of the Gospel According to St. John. I understand this Logos to be divine wisdom and love. Freud and I push Logos toward the same goals, which I would like to place on the side of the creation of positive inner and outer goods.

It is not the confession of being religious that demarcates who is a true Christian. John 13:35 gives another: "By this shall all men know that ye are my disciples, if ye have love one to another."

Despite the danger of being laughed at for having a loose tongue, I dare assert once more that Freud is, by this measure, ahead of many church-going Christians, who regard him, as he does himself, as a heathen.

And thus *The Future of an Illusion* and "The Illusion of a Future" combine in a strong faith, whose credo is: "The truth shall make you free!"

Comparing the King James Version of 1611 to the New Revised Standard Version Bible of 1989:

The highway of the upright is to depart from evil; he that keepeth his way preserveth his **soul**.

(KJV: Proverbs 16:17)

The highway of the upright avoids evil; those who guard their way preserve their **lives**.

(NRSV: Proverbs 16:17)

Appendix B:
King James Compared to *NRSV*

Table 1
How Every "Soul" in the *KJV*
Was Translated in the *NRSV*

This Table shows every occurrence of the word "soul" in the *King James Version of the Bible*. The verses are divided into two columns: the left shows those verses in which the *New Revised Standard Version* (NRSV) did not use the word "soul." The right column shows those verses in which the *New Revised Standard* did use the word "soul."

NRSV Verse:

No Mention of "Soul":	Mentions the "Soul":
Genesis	**Genesis**
2:7; 12:5,13; 17:14; 19:20; 27:4,19,25,31; 34:8; 42:21; 46:15,18,22,25-27; 49:6	34:3; 35:18
Exodus	**Exodus**
1:5; 12:4,15,19; 30:12,15,16; 31:14	none
Leviticus	**Leviticus**
4:2; 5:1,2,4,15,17; 6:2; 7:18,	none

NRSV Verse:

No Mention of "Soul":	Mentions the "Soul":
20,21,25,27; 16:29,31; 17:10-12,15; 18:29; 19:8; 20:6,25; 22:3,6,11; 23:27,29,30,32; 26:11,15,30,43	
Numbers 9:13; 11:6; 15:27,28,30,31; 16:38; 19:13,20,22; 21:4,5; 29:7; 30:2,4-13; 31:28,50	**Numbers** none
Deuteronomy 4:9; 12:15,20,21; 13:6; 14:26	**Deuteronomy** 4:29; 6:5; 10:12; 11:13,18; 13:3; 26:16; 30:2,6,10
Joshua 10:28,30,32,35,37,39; 11:11	**Joshua** 22:5; 23:14
Judges 10:16; 16:16	**Judges** 5:21
1 Samuel 1:10,26; 2:16; 17:55; 20:3,4, 17; 23:20; 24:11; 25:26,29; 26:21; 30:6	**1 Samuel** 1:15; 18:1,3
2 Samuel 4:9; 5:8; 14:19	**2 Samuel** 1:11
1 Kings 1:29; 17:21,22	**1 Kings** 2:4; 8:48; 11:37
2 Kings 2:2,4,6; 4:27,30	**2 Kings** 23:3,25

NRSV Verse:

No Mention of "Soul":	Mentions the "Soul":
1 Chronicles	**1 Chronicles**
22:19	none
2 Chronicles	**2 Chronicles**
none	6:38; 15:12; 34:31
Job	**Job**
6:7; 7:15; 9:21; 12:10; 14:22;	3:20; 7:11; 10:1; 21:25;
16:4; 19:2; 23:13; 24:12; 27:8;	27:2; 30:16,25; 33:18,22,
31:30; 33:20	28,30
Psalms	**Psalms**
3:2; 6:4; 7:2; 11:1; 16:10; 17:13;	6:3; 7:5; 11:5; 13:2; 19:7;
22:29; 25:13,20; 26:9; 31:7; 34:22;	22:20; 23:3; 24:4; 25:1;
35:4,7,13,17; 40:14; 41:4; 44:25;	30:3; 31:9; 33:19,20; 34:2;
49:8,18; 54:3,4; 55:18; 56:6; 57:4;	35:3,9,12; 42:1,2,4-6,11;
59:3; 63:9; 66:9,16; 69:1,18; 70:2;	43:5; 49:15; 56:13; 57:1,6;
71:10,13; 72:13,14; 78:50; 86:2,14;	62:1,5; 63:1,5,8; 69:10;
88:14; 89:48; 94:21; 97:10; 106:15;	71:23; 74:19; 77:2; 84:2;
107:9,18,26; 109:20,31; 116:4;	86:4,13; 88:3; 94:17,19;
119:109,175; 120:2,6; 121:7; 124:4,5,7;	103:1,2,22; 104:1,35;
139:14; 141:8; 142:4,7; 143:3,11,12	107:5; 116:7-8; 119:20,25,
	28,81,129,167; 123:4;
	130:5-6; 131:2; 138:3;
	143:6,8; 146:1
Proverbs	**Proverbs**
6:30,32; 8:36; 10:3; 11:17,25,30;	2:10; 3:22; 13:19; 16:24;
13:2,3,4,8,25; 14:25; 15:32; 16:17;	21:10; 24:12,14; 25:25
18:7; 19:2,8,15,16,18; 20:2; 21:23;	
22:5,23,25; 23:14; 25:13; 27:7;	
29:10,17,24	

NRSV Verse:

No Mention of "Soul":	Mentions the "Soul":
Ecclesiastes 2:24; 4:8; 6:2,3; 7:28	**Ecclesiastes** none
Song of Solomon 6:12	**Song of Solomon** 1:7; 3:1-4; 5:6
Isaiah 3:9; 29:8; 32:6; 38:17; 44:20; 51:23; 53:10,11,12; 55:2,3; 58:3,5,10,11; 61:10; 66:3	**Isaiah** 1:14; 10:18; 26:8,9; 38:15; 42:1
Jeremiah 2:34; 4:10,19,31; 5:9,29; 6:8; 9:9; 12:7; 14:19; 18:20; 20:13; 26:19; 31:12,14,25; 38:16,17,20; 44:7; 50:19; 51:6,45	**Jeremiah** 6:16; 13:17; 32:41
Lamentations 1:11,16,19; 2:12; 3:58	**Lamentations** 3:17,20,24,25
Ezekiel 3:19,21; 4:14; 7:19; 13:18-20; 14:14, 20; 18:4,20,27; 22:25,27; 24:21; 33:5,9	**Ezekiel** none
Hosea 9:4	**Hosea** none
Micah 7:1	**Micah** 6:7
Habakkuk 2:4,10	**Habakkuk** none

NRSV Verse:

No Mention of "Soul":	Mentions the "Soul":
Zechariah	**Zechariah**
11:8	none

Apocrypha

Tobit	**Tobit**
none	13:7,15
Judith	**Judith**
4:9; 7:27; 12:4	none
Wisdom	**Wisdom**
11:26; 12:6	1:4,11; 2:22; 3:1,13; 4:11,14; 7:27; 9:15; 10:7,16; 14:11,26; 15:11; 16:14; 17:1,8
Sirach	**Sirach**
1:30; 2:1,17; 4:2,17,20,22; 6:2,4; 7:11; 9:2,6; 10:9,28,29; 14:4,16; 16:17; 19:4; 20:22; 21:2,27,28; 25:2; 30:23; (32:23; 33:31; 34:15;) the numbers in parentheses sometimes have a different number sequence: (35:23; 30:31; 31:15, 17;) 37:27,28; 47:15; 48:5; 51:24	4:6; 7:21,29; 14:9; 18:31; (34:17); 51:6,19-20,26,29
Baruch	**Baruch**
2:17	2:18; 3:1
Epistle of Jeremiah	**Epistle of Jeremiah**
1:7	none

NRSV Verse:

No Mention of "Soul":   Mentions the "Soul":

Azarias   Azariah
none   1:64

1 Maccabees   1 Maccabees
1:48   none

2 Maccabees   2 Maccabees
none   6:30

2 Esdras   2 Esdras
3:5   3:29; 4:35,41; 5:22; 6:37;
                               7:32; 8:4; 10:36; 12:8;
                               15:8

New Testament

Matthew   Matthew
16:26; 26:38   10:28; 11:29; 12:18; 22:37

Mark   Mark
8:36,37; 12:33; 14:34   12:30

Luke   Luke
12:20   1:46; 2:35; 10:27; 12:19;
                               21:19

John   John
none   12:27

Acts   Acts
2:31,41,43; 3:23; 7:14; 15:24; 27:37   2:27; 4:32; 14:22

NRSV Verse:

No Mention of "Soul":	Mentions the "Soul":
Romans 2:9; 13:1	Romans none
1 Corinthians 15:45	1 Corinthians none
2 Corinthians 1:23	2 Corinthians none
1 Thessalonians 2:8	1 Thessalonians 5:23
Hebrews 10:39	Hebrews 4:12; 6:19; 10:38; 13:17
James none	James 1:21; 5:20
1 Peter 3:20; 4:19	1 Peter 1:9,22; 2:11,25
2 Peter none	2 Peter 2:8,14
3 John none	3 John 1:2
Revelation 16:3; 18:13	Revelation 6:9; 18:14; 20:4

Table 2
Additional Information
About the NRSV

Verses where the NRSV used the word "soul" despite the absence of the Hebrew word *nephesh* in the original text:

Deuteronomy
10:13,18; 13:3

Psalms
16:9; 30:12; 34:6; 57:8;
73:21; 108:1; 23:16

Isaiah
16:11; 57:16

Verses where the Hebrew *nephesh* was not translated into "soul" in the KJV, but was in the NRSV:

Proverbs
27:9

Isaiah
15:4

Ezekiel
27:31

Verses where the Greek *psyche* was not translated into "soul" in the KJV, but was in the NRSV:

Tobit
13:6

Wisdom
8:19; 9:3; 15:8; 17:15

Sirach
6:26; 31:28; 45:23; 50:25

2 Maccabees
3:16; 15:17,30;

4 Maccabees
1:20,26,28; 3:15; 13:21; 15:25; 18:23

And he stretched himself upon the child three times, and cried unto the Lord, and said, O Lord my God, I pray thee, let this child's **soul** come into him again. And the Lord heard the voice of Elijah; and the **soul** of the child came into him again, and he revived.

(KJV: 1 Kings 17:21-22)

Then he stretched himself upon the child three times, and cried out to the Lord, "O Lord my God, let this child's **life** come into him again." The Lord listened to the voice of elijah; the **life** of the child came into him again, and he revived.

(NRSV: 1 Kings 17:21-22)

Endnotes

Chapter 1
Soul Murder

1. Henrik Ibsen, "John Gabriel Borkman," trans. W. Archer, in *Collected Works*, New York: Scribner's, 1926, vol. 11, pp. 179-353. On p. 268, Ella Rentheim says, "You are guilty of a double murder — the murder of your own soul, and mine."

2. Leonard Shengold, *Soul Murder: The Effects of Childhood Abuse and Deprivation*, New Haven: Yale University Press, 1989.

3. The battle of the "Resurrectionists" was led by Oscar Cullmann against the "Immortalists" who held the view that the soul is immortal as Plato had said. Parts of this battle can be found in: Cullmann, *Immortality of the Soul or Resurrection of the Dead?*, New York: MacMillan & Co., 1958; Krister Stendahl, "Immortality Is Too Much and Too Little," in Stendahl, *Meanings: The Bible as Document and Guide*, Minneapolis: Augsburg Fortress Press, 1984, pp. 193-202; Stendahl ed., *Immortality and Resurrection*, New York: MacMillan & Co., 1958; and John Hick, *Death and Eternal Life*, New York: Harper & Row, 1976.

4. Margaret S. Mahler, Fred Pine, and Anni Bergman, *The Psychological Birth of the Human Infant: Symbiosis and Individuation*, New York: Basic Books, 1975.

5. A relationship between borderline personality disorder and child abuse has been established in a number of research studies: Charles P. Barnard and Cynthia Hirsch, "Borderline Personality and Victims of Incest,"

Psychological Reports 1985; 57: 715-18; Jeffrey B. Bryer et al, "Childhood Sexual and Physical Abuse as Factors in Adult Psychiatric Illness," *American Journal of Psychiatry* 1987; 144:1426-30; Judith L. Herman, Christopher Perry, and Bessel A. Van der Kolk, "Childhood Trauma in Borderline Personality Disorder," *American Journal of Psychiatry* 1989; 146:490-95; Michaela Kauffmann, "Relationship Between Child Maltreatment/Sexual Abuse, Borderline Personality Disorder, and Post-Traumatic Stress Disorder" (Psy.D. thesis, University of Hartford, 1992); Susan N. Ogata et al, "Childhood Sexual and Physical Abuse in Adult Patients with Borderline Personality Disorder," *American Journal of Psychiatry* 1990; 147: 1008-13; Helen Sheldon, "Childhood Sexual Abuse in Adult Female Psychotherapy Referrals," *British Journal of Psychiatry* 1988; 152: 107-11; Van der Kolk, *Psychological Trauma*, Washington: American Psychiatric Press, 1987.

Chapter 2
Comment by Krister Stendahl

6. Stendahl, *Paul Among Jews & Gentiles & Other Essays*, Minneapolis: Augsburg Fortress Press, 1976:

> Such a doctrine of justification by faith was hammered out by Paul for the very specific and limited purpose of defending the rights of the Gentile converts to be full and genuine heirs to the promises of God to Israel . . . . We think that Paul spoke about justification by faith, using the Jewish-Gentile situation as an instance, as an example. But Paul was chiefly concerned about the relation between Jews and Gentiles — and in the development of *this* concern he used as one of his arguments the idea of justification by faith. (pp. 2-3)
>
> It is very important, for example, that when Paul speaks about the Jews, he really speaks about Jews, and not simply the fantasy Jews who stand as a symbol or as the prime example of a timeless legalism. (pp. 36-37)

Stendahl's view that Justification by Faith meant to Paul something different than what Martin Luther thought Paul was saying, has been widely accepted by Bible scholars. See also Stendahl, "The Apostle Paul and the Introspective Conscience of the West," *Harvard Theological Review* 1963; 56: 199-215.

Chapter 4
Quenton Hyder, M.D.

7. Phone conversations with Quenton Hyder November 1991, and May 17 and October 25, 1992.

8. In the Bible, dreams may have been the primary channel through which people heard God speaking. This is why prophets were called "seers," because they saw dreams and visions.

Old Testament dreams:

Genesis	20:3-7; 28:10-22; 31:10-13,24; 32:22-32; 37:5-11,19-20; 40:1-42:9
Numbers	12:4-8
Deuteronomy	13:1-5
Judges	7:13-15
1 Samuel	28:6,15
2 Samuel	7:4-17
1 Kings	3:5-15
1 Chronicles	17:3-15
Job	4:12-15; 7:13-15; 20:8; 33:14-16
Psalms	73:18-20; 126:1-2
Ecclesiastes	5:3,7
Isaiah	29:7-11
Jeremiah	23:25,32; 27:9-10; 29:8-9
Daniel	1:17; 2:1-48; 4:5-28; 5:12-13; 7:1-2f
Joel	2:28
Zechariah	10:2

Apocrypha dreams:

2 Esdras	10:36; 11:1f; 12:35; 13:1-19,53; 14:8
Rest of Esther	10:5; 11:2-12
Wisdom	18:17,19
Sirach	34:1-7
2 Maccabees	15:11

New Testament dreams:

Matthew	1:20-23; 2:12-15,19,22; 27:19
Acts	2:17; 16:9-10; 18:9-11; 23:11; 27:23-25

Visions in the Bible (usually visions at night):

Old Testament visions:

Genesis	15:1; 46:2-4
Numbers	12:4-8; 24:4,16
Joshua	5:13-15
1 Samuel	3:1-16
2 Chronicles	9:29; 32:32
Job	7:13-15; 20:8; 33:14-16
Psalms	89:19-21f
Proverbs	29:18
Isaiah	1:1-2f; 13:1; 21:1-3; 22:1,5; 28:7; 29:7
Jeremiah	14:14; 23:16
Lamentations	2:9
Ezekiel	1:1; 7:13,26; 8:3-4; 11:24-25; 12:21-27; 13:7,16; 40:2; 43:1-3 (Note that verse 1:1 implies that the entire chapter is a vision.)

Daniel	1:17; 2:19,28; 4:5-13f; 7:1-8:27; 9:20-27; 10:1,7-11:1,14
Hosea	12:10
Joel	2:28-31
Obadiah	1:1
Micah	3:5-7
Nahum	1:1f
Habakkuk	2:2-3
Zechariah	10:2; 13:4

Apocrypha visions:

2 Esdras	10:37,40,59; 12:8-11; 13:21,25; 14:18,42; 15:28
Tobit	12:19
Wisdom	17:4; 18:17
Sirach	34:3; 40:6; 46:15; 48:22; 49:8
2 Maccabees	15:12

New Testament visions:

Luke	1:11-22; 24:4-11,23
Acts	2:17; 9:3-19; 10:1-23; 11:4-18; 12:9; 16:9-10; 18:9-11; 26:12-19
2 Corinthians	12:1
Revelation	1:1; 9:17 (Note that verse 1:1 implies that the entire chapter is a vision.)

This topic is discussed in the Glossary of the author's book *Soul Psychology*. See also references on the biblical emphasis on dreams and visions: I. Mendelsohn, "Dreams," in George A. Buttrick et al, eds., *The Interpreter's Dictionary of the Bible: An Illustrated Encyclopedia*, Nashville: Abingdon Press, 1981, vol. 1, pp. 868-69; B. D. Napier, "Visions," vol. 4, p. 791; A. L. Oppenheim, "The Interpretation of Dreams in the Ancient Near East with a Translation of an Assyrian Dream Book," *Transactions of the American Philosophical Society* 1956; 46: 3.

Chapter 5
Comment by Krister Stendahl

9. Stendahl, *Meanings: The Bible as Document and Guide*, Minneapolis: Augsburg Fortress Press, 1984.

Chapter 6
Dan Blazer, M.D., Ph.D.

10. Telephone interviews with Dan Blazer, November 14 and December 10, 1991; May 17 and October 25, 1992.

11. Dr. Blazer misquoted the article in a humorous way. Actually the title is not "Is Psychiatry Losing Its Mind?" but Morton F. Reiser, "Are Psychiatric

Educators 'Losing the Mind?'" *American Journal of Psychiatry* 1988; 145: 148-53.

12. Marian Wright Edelman, *The Measure of Our Success: A Letter to My Children and Yours*, Boston: Beacon Press, 1992.

13. Hans Küng, *Freud and the Problem of God*, New Haven: Yale University Press, 1990.

Chapter 7
Sally

14. Letter from Sally, March 24, 1993.

Chapter 8
Susan Leigh Deppe, M.D.

15. Phone conversations with Susan Leigh Deppe, M.D., November 20, 1991, April 20, 1993 and May, 1993, and personal communications May 20 and June 17, 1993.

16. Leslie D. Weatherhead, *The Will of God*, Nashville: Abingdon Press, 1976; John B. Phillips, *Your God Is Too Small*, New York: MacMillan, 1964; Harold S. Kushner, *When Bad Things Happen to Good People*, New York: Avon Publishers, 1983; Morton T. Kelsey, *Encounter With God*, Minneapolis: Bethany Fellowship, 1972; M. Scott Peck, *The Road Less Travelled*, New York: Simon & Schuster, 1988.

17. The American Psychiatric Association has officially issued ethical guidelines that "psychiatrists should maintain respect for their patients' beliefs," and "should not impose their own religious, antireligious or ideological systems of beliefs on their patients . . . ." American Psychiatric Association, "Guidelines Regarding Possible Conflict Between Psychiatrists' Religious Commitments and Psychiatric Practice," *American Journal of Psychiatry*, 1990; 147: 542.

18.   The Lord is my light and my salvation; whom shall I fear? The Lord is the stronghold of my life; of whom shall I be afraid? When evildoes assail me to devour my flesh — my adversaries and foes — they shall stumble and fall (NRSV: Psalm 27:1-2).

19. John 13:36-38; 18:15-18,25-27; 21:15-17.

20. Matthew 28:1-10; Mark 5:24-34; 16:1-8; Luke 24:1-11; John 4:4-30; 20:10-18. Jesus also dealt with women more respectfully than did his patriarchal culture.

21. M. O. Vincent, "Christianity and Psychiatry: Rivals or Allies?" *Canadian Psychiatric Association Journal*, 1975; 20:528.

Chapter 9
David Larson, M.D., M.S.P.H.

22. David B. Larson et al, "The Couch and the Cloth: The Need for Linkage," *Hospital and Community Psychiatry 1988*; 39: 1064-69.

23. Larson and Susan S. Larson, *The Forgotten Factor in Physical and Mental Health: What Does the Research Show?*, Arlington, Va: National Institute for Healthcare Research, 1992. Copies are available from 2111 Wilson Boulevard, Suite 1130, Arlington, VA 22201, or call (703) 527-NIHR, or FAX (703) 527-3160.

24. Phone conversations with David Larson, November 15 and December 3 and 6, 1991.

25. Ernest Becker, *Denial of Death*, New York: MacMillan, 1975.

26. W. E. Henry, J. H. Sims, and S. L. Spray, *The Fifth Profession*, San Francisco: Jossey-Bass, 1971, pp. 45-71.

27. Larson et al, "Systematic Analysis of Research on Religious Variables in Four Major Psychiatric Journals, 1978-1982," *American Journal of Psychiatry* 1986; 143: 329-34.

28. David R. Williams et al, "Religion and Psychological Distress in a Community Sample," *Social Science and Medicine*, 1991; 32: 1257-62.

29. Larson et al, "Systematic Analysis of Research on Religious Variables."

30. George E. Vaillant and Eva S. Milofsky, "Natural History of Male Alcoholism: IV. Paths to Recovery," *Archives of General Psychiatry* 1982; 39: 127-33. Table 4, p. 130, shows that abstinence from alcohol was significantly associated with increased religious involvement, and also significantly associated with Alcoholics Anonymous. In the text on p. 130 (lower left), this is classified as a "substitute dependency" similar to candy binges and assorted compulsions.

31. James F. Maddux and David P. Desmond, "Residence Relocation Inhibits Opioid Dependence," *Archives of General Psychiatry* 1982; 39: 1313-17. See Table 1 on p. 1315 which shows that 43% of those abstinent were in a religious program, compared to 19% who relocated their residence. It was the latter datum which became the focus of the article the authors wrote, not the former and more important religious factor. The religious factor is discussed in passing, and dismissed, on p. 1314 in the lower right corner.

32. Edward Gottheil, Ralph V. Exline, and Richard Winkelmayer, "Judging Emotions of Normal and Schizophrenic Subjects," *American Journal of Psychiatry* 1979; 136: 1049-54. Table 2 on p. 1052 shows the largest R-squared was associated with religious activities. This is mentioned in passing in the results section (p. 1052 bottom left) and the discussion section (p. 1053 middle of right column), but only in passing. No discussion of the meaning of these religious data is offered.

33. Bruce Greyson and Ian Stevenson, "The Phenomenology of Near-Death Experiences," *American Journal of Psychiatry* 1980; 137: 1193-96. Table 1 on p. 1194 shows that 37% of the sample had a prior sense of God within oneself, and another 50% had a sense of unity with nature. This is vastly greater than the general population, of which 28% had one of these two experiences. However, this remarkable difference is not discussed in the text. Table 2 on p. 1195 shows the size of the changes.

34. Jerome A. Motto, "The Psychopathology of Suicide: A Clinical Model Approach," *American Journal of Psychiatry* 1979; 136: 516-20. Table 2 on p. 517 shows that a low or moderate degree of religious activity is a significant predictor of suicide. Table 3 on p. 518 again shows a significant relationship between absence of religion and subsequent suicide. These facts are not discussed in the text.

35. Kathryn Anastos et al, "Hypertension in Women: What Really Is Known? The Women's Caucus, Working Group on Women's Heath of the Society of General Internal Medicine," *Annals of Internal Medicine* 1991; 115: 287-93; and Jerry H. Gurwitz, Nananda F. Col, and Jerry Avorn, "The Exclusion of the Elderly and Women from Clinical Trials in Acute Myocardial Infarction," *Journal of the American Medical Association* 1992; 268: 1417-22.

Chapter 11
John Young, M.D.

36. Numerous conversations by phone and face-to-face between 1989 and 1993.

37. Jeffrey H. Boyd, *Soul Psychology: How to Understand Your Soul In Light of the Mental Health Movement*, Prospect, Conn: Soul Research Institute, forthcoming. See the order form at the end of this book.

38. Ira Progoff, *Cloud of Unknowing*, New York: Doubleday, 1989.

Chapter 12
Louisa Mattson, Ph.D.

39. Telephone interview with Louisa Mattson, December 7, 1992.

40. Thomas Moore, *Care of the Soul*, New York: Harper Collins, 1992.

41. This is discussed at length in the author's forthcoming book, *Soul Psychology*.

42. Alan Jones, *Soul Making*, San Francisco: Harper San Francisco, 1989.

43. John Seed, *Thinking Like a Mountain: Toward a Council of All Being*, Philadelphia: New Society Education Foundation, 1988.

Chapter 13
Larry Schulte, Ph.D.

44. Telephone conversations with Larry Schulte, November 13 and 20, 1991; May 17 and October 26, 1992.

45. Abraham Maslow, *Motivation and Personality*, New York: Harper & Row, 1970, pp. 97-104.

46. Irvin D. Yalom, *Love's Executioner and Other Tales of Psychotherapy*, New York: Harper Collins, 1990.

Chapter 15
What Is a Human Being?

47. American Psychiatric Association, *Diagnostic and Statistical Manual, rev. 3rd ed.*, Washington: American Psychiatric Association Press, 1987. The author is a contributor to the section on anxiety disorders.

48. Boyd, "The Increasing Rate of Suicide by Firearms," *New England Journal of Medicine* 1983; 308: 872-74; "In Response to Letters to the Editor," 1984; 310: 48-49; and Robert A. Ostroff and Boyd, "Television and Suicide," 1987; 316: 876-77.

49. Dante Alighieri, *The Divine Comedy*, trans. Jefferson Butler Fletcher, New York: Columbia University Press, 1931, Canto 1.

50. Augustine, *Saint Augustine Confessions*, trans. R. S. Pine-Coffin, New York: Penguin Books, 1987.

51. Boyd, *Soul Psychology*.

52. Mahler, Pine, and Bergman, *The Psychological Birth of the Human Infant*.

53. Donald W. Winnicott, *Home Is Where We Start From*, Clare Winnicott, Ray Shepherd, and Madeleine Davis, eds., New York: W. W. Norton, 1986; *Playing and Reality*, New York: Routledge, 1989; *Through Paediatrics to Psycho-Analysis*, New York: Basic Books, 1975, pp. 97-100; Davis and David Wallbridge, *Boundary and Space: An Introduction to the Work of D. W. Winnicott*, New York: Brunner Mazel, 1990.

54. John McDargh, *Psychoanalytic Object Relations Theory and the Study of Religion: On Faith and the Imaging of God*, Lanham, Md.: University Press of America, 1983.

55. Jean Piaget, "The Construction of Reality in the Child," in Howard E. Gruber and J. Jacques Vonèche, eds., *The Essential Piaget*, New York: Basic Books, 1977, pp. 254-55. See also pp. 250-72. Originally translated by Margaret Cook, and published as *The Construction of Reality in the Child*, New York: Basic Books, 1954.

56. Winnicott, "Transitional Objects and Transitional Phenomena," *The International Journal of Psychoanalysis* 1953; 34(2): 89-97.

57. Augustine, p. 48.

Chapter 16
One Soul in Depth

58. American Psychiatric Association, *Psychiatrists' Viewpoints on Religion and Their Services to Religious Institutions and the Ministry*, Task Force Report 10, Washington: American Psychiatric Association, 1975; and Claude Ragan, H. Newton Malony, and Benjamin Bert-Hallahmi, "Psychologists and Religion:

Professional Factors and Personal Belief," *Review of Religious Research* 1980; 21: 208-17. Table 2 on p. 212 shows that 17% of psychologists were "orthodox" in ideology and another 26% somewhat orthodox. At the bottom of the page the text adds together these two percentages, and arrives at 43% believing in God. The article shows that psychologists are much less religious than academics in general, or the American public.

    Larson et al, in "Systematic Analysis of Research," on p. 329 incorrectly quote an unpublished study of Regan et al in 1976 that found 5% of psychologists in the APA believe in God.

59. Gallup Poll, *Religion in America, Gallup Report* #259, April 1987.

60. Azariah: Song of Three Young Men 1:40-51, from the *Apocrypha, King James Version.*

61. Thomas Merton introduced into religion the idea of the "False Self," which also is an idea that has played a major role in the writing of Donald Winnicott: Thomas Merton, *Honorable Reader: Reflections on My Work*, New York: Crossroad Publishing, 1981, pp. 133-34; Anne Carr, "Transformations of the Self in Thomas Merton," address delivered at Marquard Chapel, Yale Divinity School, February 1, 1989; Winnicott, *Playing and Reality, Home Is Where We Start From*, and *Through Paediatrics to Psycho-Analysis.*

62. Martha L. Rogers, ed., "Satanic Ritual Abuse: The Current State of Knowledge," *Journal of Psychology and Theology*, 1992; 20 (3): 175-339.

Chapter 17
The "Soul" and Sigmund Freud

63. Karl Barth, "The Doctrine of Creation," *Church Dogmatics*, 13 books (which Barth calls "5 vols."), G. W. Bromiley and T.F. Torrance, eds., Harold Knight et al, trans., Edinburgh: T. & T. Clark Publishers, 1960, vol. 3, pt. 4, sec. 54, pp. 135-56. Karl Barth said that Sigmund Freud was talking about the soul. Barth thought Freud vastly overemphasized sexuality as if sexuality were the core of the soul.

64. Bruno Bettelheim, "Reflections: Freud and the Soul," *The New Yorker*, March 1, 1982, pp. 52-93 (see especially p. 86); and Bettelheim, *Freud and Man's Soul*, New York: Random House, 1984, p. 74.

65. Sigmund Freud, *"Psychische Behandlung (Seelenbehandlung)"*, in *Die Gesundheit: Ihre Erhaltung, ihre Störungen, ihre Wiederherstellung*, 2 vols., Robby A. Kossmann and Jul. Weiss, eds., Stuttgart: Union Deutsche Verlagsgesellschaft, 1905, vol. 1, pp. 368-84.

66. Peter Terrell et al, *Collins German-English, English-German Dictionary*, p. 599.

67. Freud, "Psychical (or Mental) Treatment," *The Standard Edition of the Complete Psychological Works of Sigmund Freud*, 24 vols., James Strachey, trans., London: Hogarth Press, 1986, vol. 7, p. 283.

68. W. W. Meissner, *Psychoanalysis and Religious Experience*, New Haven: Yale University Press, 1984, p. 74.

69. Freud and Oskar Pfister, *Psychoanalysis and Faith: The Letters of Sigmund Freud and Oskar Pfister*, Heinrich Meng and Ernst L. Freud, eds., Eric Mosbacher, trans., New York: Basic Books, 1963, p. 63, letter to Freud of October 29, 1918.

70. Ibid., p. 120, letter to Freud, February 20, 1928.

71. Ibid., p. 142, letter to Pfister, November 25, 1934.

72. Ibid., p. 106, letter to Pfister, November 21, 1926.

73. Anna Freud, Preface, in *Psychoanalysis and Faith*, p. 11.

74. Freud-Pfister letters, p. 94, letter to Pfister, November 5, 1924.

75. G. Stanley Hall, Introduction, in Pfister, *The Psychoanalytic Method*, Charles Rockwell Payne, trans., New York: Moffat, Yard & Co., p. ix.

76. Freud, Introduction, in Pfister, *The Psychoanalytic Method*, pp. v-viii.

77. Freud, "The Future of an Illusion," in *The Standard Edition*, 21: 38.

78. Ibid., pp. 5-56.

79. Freud-Pfister letters, p. 130, letter to Pfister, May 26, 1929.

80. Ibid., pp. 112-13, letter to Pfister, October 22, 1927.

81. Ibid., p. 122, letter to Pfister, February 24, 1928; see also p. 117, letter to Pfister, November 26, 1927.

82. Freud, "Civilization and Its Discontents," in *The Standard Edition*, 21: 82.

83. Ibid., p. 74.

84. Ibid., p. 76.

85. Ibid., p. 76.

86. Freud, "The Question of a Weltanschauung," in *The Standard Edition*, 22: 158-82.

87. Erich Fromm, *Psychoanalysis and Religion*, New Haven: Yale University Press, 1950.

88. Ibid., pp. 65-98.

89. Lillian Robinson, ed., *Psychiatry and Religion: Overlapping Concerns*, Washington: American Psychiatric Press, 1986.

90. Meissner, pp. 57-72.

91. Freud-Pfister letters, p. 104, letter to Freud, September 10, 1926.

92. Ibid., p. 99, letter to Freud, October 8, 1925.

Chapter 18
Comment by Stendahl

93. Richard Gombrich, "Introduction: The Buddhist Way," in Heinz Bechert and Gombrich, eds., *The World of Buddhism*, London: Thames & Hudson, 1991, pp. 9-14; and Etienne Lamotte, "The Buddha: His Teachings and His Sangha," pp. 42-47.

94. That the word "self" is a synonym of the word "soul" is evident when we compare the King James Version to the New Revised Standard Version Bible in these verses:

> Though I were perfect, yet would I not know my **soul**. (KJV: Job 9:21)
> I am blameless; I do not know my**self**. (NRSV: Job 9:21)

> So being affectionately desirous of you, we were willing to have imparted unto you, not the gospel of God only, but also our own **souls**, because ye were dear unto us. (KJV: 1 Thessalonians 2:8)
> So deeply do we care for you that we are determined to share with you not only the gospel of God but also our own **selves**, because you have become very dear to us. (NRSV: 1 Thessalonians 2:8)

But his flesh upon him shall have pain, and his **soul** within him shall mourn. (KJV: Job 14:22)
They feel only the pain of their own bodies, and mourn only for themselves. (NRSV: Job 14:22)

95. Kohut's viewpoint is explained and compared with a Christian viewpoint in the author's book, *Soul Psychology*.

96. Matthew 3:3; 7:13-14; Mark 1:2-3; Luke 1:79; 7:27; John 14:4-6; Acts 16:17; 18:25-26; 22:4; 24:14; Romans 3:17; 1 Corinthians 12:31; 1 Thessalonians 3:11; Hebrews 10:20; 2 Peter 2:2,15.

97. Psalm 1:1,5-6; 16:11; 23:1-4.

98. Matthew 6:33; 7:7-8; 13:45; 28:5; Mark 1:37; Luke 11:9-10; 12:29-31; 13:24; 15:8; 17:33; 19:10; 24:5; John 1:38; 4:23,27; 5:44; 8:21,50; 13:33; 18:4,7-8; Acts 15:17; 17:27; Romans 2:7; 3:11; 11:7; 1 Corinthians 14:12; Philippians 2:21; Colossians 3:1; Hebrews 11:6; 13:14.

Appendix: "Illusion of a Future" by Pastor Oskar Pfister

99. Pfister, "The Illusion of a Future: A Friendly Discussion with Prof. Dr. Sigmund Freud," Ted Crump and Jeffrey H. Boyd, trans. Crump is at the National Institutes of Health Library. This essay was published in German in 1928 ("*Die Illusion einer Zukunft: Eine freundschaftliche Auseinandersetzung mit Prof. Dr. Sigm. Freud*," *Imago* 1928; 14(2/3): 149-184). *Imago* was published from 1912 to 1937, and then went out of existence. It was partly folded into the *Internationale Zeitschrift für Pychoanalyse und Imago*, which ceased publication in 1941. The Nazis had taken over Germany, and they were both anti-Semitic and hostile to psychoanalysis.

In this translation, the numbers have been omitted from the text referencing the pages of Freud's original booklet *The Future of an Illusion*, because those page numbers are no longer relevant to reprints of Freud's essay. The word "soul" has been set in bold, whereas it was not in bold in Pfister's German.

100. Pfister's idea of "the world will" as his way of denoting "God" may have come from Arthur Schopenhauer's book *The World as Will and Idea*. Schopenhauer had a major influence on Freud as shown in Strachey,

"Appendix to Freud's Essay 'Resistances to Psycho-Analysis,'" in *The Standard Edition*, 19: 223-24; and Freud, "An Autobiographical Study," 20:59.

101.   Constantin Meunier was a Nineteenth Century Belgian sculptor.

Comparing the King James Version of 1611 to the New Revised Standard Version Bible of 1989:

Be thou instructed, O Jerusalem, lest my **soul** depart from thee; lest I make thee desolate, a land not inhabited.

(KJV: Jeremiah 6:8)

Take warning, O Jerusalem or I shall turn from you in disgust, and make you a desolation, an uninhabited land.

(NRSV: Jeremiah 6:8)

Bibliography

Alighieri, Dante. *The Divine Comedy.* Translated by Jefferson Butler Fletcher. New York: Columbia University Press, 1931.

American Psychiatric Association. "Guidelines Regarding Possible Conflict Between Psychiatrists' Religious Commitments and Psychiatric Practice." *American Journal of Psychiatry*, 1990; 147: 542.

_____. *Psychiatrists' Viewpoints on Religion and Their Services to Religious Institutions and the Ministry.* Task Force Report 10. Washington: American Psychiatric Association, 1975.

Anastos, Kathryn, Pamela Charney, Rita A. Charon, Ellen Cohen, Clara Y. Jones, Carola Marte, Deborah M. Swiderski, Mary E. Wheat, and Sarah Williams. "Hypertension in Women: What Really Is Known? The Women's Caucus, Working Group on Women's Heath of the Society of General Internal Medicine." *Annals of Internal Medicine*, 1991; 115: 287-93.

Augustine, Saint. *Confessions.* Translated by R. S. Pine-Coffin. New York: Penguin Books, 1987.

Barnard, Charles P., and Cynthia Hirsch. "Borderline Personality and Victims of Incest." *Psychological Reports* 1985; 57: 715-18.

Barth, Karl. *Church Dogmatics*, 13 books (which Barth calls "5 vols."). Edited by G. W. Bromiley and T.F. Torrance. Translated by Harold Knight, G.W. Bromiley, J.K.S. Reid, and R. H. Fuller. Edinburgh: T. & T. Clark Publishers, 1960.

Becker, Ernest. *Denial of Death*. New York: MacMillan, 1975.

Bettelheim, Bruno. *Freud and Man's Soul*. New York: Random House, 1984.

_____. "Reflections: Freud and the Soul." *The New Yorker*, March 1, 1982, pp. 52-93.

Boyd, Jeffrey H. "The Increasing Rate of Suicide by Firearms." *New England Journal of Medicine* 1983; 308: 872-74.

_____. "In Response to Letters to the Editor." *New England Journal of Medicine* 1984; 310: 48-49.

_____. *Soul Psychology: How to Understand Your Soul in Light of the Mental Health Movement*. Cheshire, Conn.: Soul Research Institute, 1994.

Bryer, Jeffrey B., Bernadette A. Nelson, Jean Baker Miller, and Pamela A. Krol. "Childhood Sexual and Physical Abuse as Factors in Adult Psychiatric Illness." *American Journal of Psychiatry* 1987; 144:1426-30.

Carr, Anne. "Transformations of the Self in Thomas Merton." Address delivered at Marquard Chapel, Yale Divinity School, February 1, 1989.

Cullmann, Oscar. *Immortality of the Soul or Resurrection of the Dead?* New York: MacMillan & Co., 1958.

Dante. See "Alighieri, Dante"

Davis, Madeleine, and David Wallbridge. *Boundary and Space: An Introduction to the Work of D. W. Winnicott*. New York: Brunner Mazel, 1990.

Edelman, Marian Wright. *The Measure of Our Success: A Letter to My Children and Yours*. Boston: Beacon Press, 1992.

Freud, Sigmund. "An Autobiographical Study." In *The Standard Edition of the Complete Psychological Works of Sigmund Freud*, 24 vols. Translated by James Strachey. London: The Hogarth Press, 1986, 20:7-76.

_____. "Civilization and Its Discontents." In *The Standard Edition*, 21:64-145.

_____. "The Future of an Illusion." In *The Standard Edition*, 21:5-56.

_____. "Introduction." In Oskar Pfister, *The Psychoanalytic Method*. Translated by Charles Rockwell Payne. New York: Moffat, Yard & Co., 1917, pp. v-viii.

_____. "Psychical (or Mental) Treatment." In *The Standard Edition*, 7:283-304.

_____. "Psychische Behandlung (Seelenbehandlung)." In *Die Gesundheit: Ihre Erhaltung, ihre Störungen, ihre Wiederherstellung*, 2 vols. Edited by Robby A. Kossmann and Jul. Weiss. Stuttgart: Union Deutsche Verlagsgesellschaft, 1905, vol. 1, pp. 368-84.

_____. "The Question of a Weltanschauung." In *The Standard Edition*, 22:158-82.

_____ and Pfister. *Psychoanalysis and Faith: The Letters of Sigmund Freud and Oskar Pfister*. Edited by Heinrich Meng and Ernst L. Freud. Translated by Eric Mosbacher. New York: Basic Books, 1963.

Fromm, Erich. *Psychoanalysis and Religion*. New Haven: Yale University Press, 1950.

Gallup Poll. *Religion in America. The Gallup Report #259*, April 1987.

Gombrich, Richard. "Introduction: The Buddhist Way." In *The World of Buddhism*. Edited by Heinz Bechert and Gombrich. London: Thames & Hudson, 1991, pp. 9-14.

Gurwitz, Jerry H., Nananda F. Col, and Jerry Avorn. "The Exclusion of the Elderly and Women from Clinical Trials in Acute Myocardial Infarction." *Journal of the American Medical Association*, 1992; 268: 1417-22.

Henry, W. E., J. H. Sims, and S. L. Spray. *The Fifth Profession*. San Francisco: Jossey-Bass, 1971.

Herman, Judith L., Christopher Perry, and Bessel A. Van der Kolk. "Childhood Trauma in Borderline Personality Disorder." *American Journal of Psychiatry*, 1989; 146: 490-95.

Hick, John. *Death and Eternal Life*. New York: Harper & Row, 1976.

Ibsen, Henrik. "John Gabriel Borkman." Translated by W. Archer. In *Collected Works*. New York: Scribner's, 1926.

Jones, Alan. *Soul Making*. San Francisco: Harper, 1989.

Kauffmann, Michaela. "Relationship Between Child Maltreatment / Sexual Abuse, Borderline Personality Disorder, and Post-Traumatic Stress Disorder." Psy.D. thesis, University of Hartford, 1992.

Kelsey, Morton T. *Encounter With God.* Minneapolis: Bethany Fellowship, 1972.

Küng, Hans. *Freud and the Problem of God.* New Haven: Yale University Press, 1990.

Kushner, Harold S. *When Bad Things Happen to Good People.* New York, Avon Books, 1983.

Lamotte, Etienne. "The Buddha: His Teachings and His Sangha." In *The World of Buddhism.* Edited by Heinz Bechert and Richard Gombrich. London: Thames & Hudson, 1991.

Larson, David B., A. A. Hohmann, Larry G. Kessler, K. G. Meador, Boyd, and E. McSherry. "The Couch and the Cloth: The Need for Linkage." *Hospital and Community Psychiatry* 1988; 39: 1064-69.

_____ and Susan S. Larson. *The Forgotten Factor in Physical and Mental Health: What Does the Research Show?* Arlington, Va: National Institute for Healthcare Research, 1992. This can be obtained from the National Institute for Healthcare Research, 2111 Wilson Boulevard, Suite 1130, Arlington, Virginia 22201, phone (703) 527-NIHR, or FAX (703) 527-3160. As of 1994 this book may be available from a publisher, so check *Books in Print.*

_____, E. Mansell Pattison, Dan G. Blazer, Abdul R. Omran, and Berton H. Kaplan. "Systematic Analysis of Research on Religious Variables in Four Major Psychiatric Journals, 1978-1982." *American Journal of Psychiatry* 1986; 143: 329-34.

McDargh, John. *Psychoanalytic Object Relations Theory and the Study of Religion: On Faith and the Imaging of God.* Lanham, Md: University Press of America, 1983.

Mahler, Margaret S., Fred Pine, and Anni Bergman. *The Psychological Birth of the Human Infant: Symbiosis and Individuation.* New York: Basic Books, 1975.

Maslow, Abraham. *Motivation and Personality.* New York: Harper & Row, 1970.

Meissner, W. W. *Psychoanalysis and Religious Experience.* New Haven: Yale University Press, 1984.

Mendelsohn, I. "Dreams." In *The Interpreter's Dictionary of the Bible: An Illustrated Encyclopedia,* 5 vols. Edited by George A. Buttrick, Thomas S. Kepler, John Knox, Herbert G. May, Samuel Terrien, and Emory S. Bucke. Nashville: Abingdon Press, 1981.

Merton, Thomas. *Honorable Reader: Reflections on My Work.* New York: Crossroad, 1981.

Moore, Thomas. *Care of the Soul.* New York: Harper Collins, 1992.

Napier, B. D. "Visions." In *The Interpreter's Dictionary of the Bible.* Nashville: Abingdon Press, 1981.

New Oxford Annotated Bible with the Apocrypha. New York: Oxford University Press, 1977.

New Revised Standard Version Bible. Nashville, Tenn., Thomas Nelson, 1990.

Ogata, Susan N., Kenneth R. Silk, Sonya Goodrich, Naomi Lohr, Drew Westen, and Elizabeth M. Hill. "Childhood Sexual and Physical Abuse in Adult Patients With Borderline Personality Disorder." *American Journal of Psychiatry* 1990; 147: 1008-13.

Oppenheim, A. L. "The Interpretation of Dreams in the Ancient Near East with a Translation of an Assyrian Dream Book." *Transactions of the American Philosophical Society* 1956; 46: 3f.

Peck, M. Scott. *The Road Less Travelled.* New York: Simon & Schuster, 1988.

Pfister, Oskar. "Die Illusion einer Zukunft: Eine freundschaftliche Auseinandersetzung mit Prof. Dr. Sigm. Freud." *Imago* 1928; 14(2/3): 149-84.

_____. *The Psychoanalytic Method.* Translated by Charles Rockwell Payne. New York: Moffat, Yard & Co., 1917.

Phillips, John B. *Your God Is Too Small.* New York: MacMillan, 1964.

Piaget, Jean. "The Construction of Reality in the Child." In *The Essential Piaget*. Edited by Howard E. Gruber and J. Jacques Vonèche. New York: Basic Books, 1977, pp. 254-55. Originally translated by Margaret Cook, *The Construction of Reality in the Child*. New York: Basic Books, 1954.

Plaskow, Judith. *Sex, Sin and Grace: Women's Experience and the Theologies of Reinhold Niebuhr and Paul Tillich*. Lanham, Md. University Press of America, 1980.

Progoff, Ira. *Cloud of Unknowing*. New York: Doubleday, 1989.

Ragan, Claude, H. Newton Malony, and Benjamin Bert- Hallahmi. "Psychologists and Religion: Professional Factors and Personal Belief." *Review of Religious Research*, Spring 1980; 21: 208-17.

Reiser, Morton F. "Are Psychiatric Educators 'Losing the Mind'?" *American Journal of Psychiatry* 1988; 145: 148-53.

Robinson, Lillian, ed. *Psychiatry and Religion: Overlapping Concerns*. Washington: American Psychiatric Press, 1986.

Rogers, Martha L., ed. "Satanic Ritual Abuse: The Current State of Knowledge." *Journal of Psychology and Theology* 1992; 20 (3): 175-339.

Seed, John. *Thinking Like a Mountain: Toward a Council of All Being*. Philadelphia: New Society Education Foundation, 1988.

Sheldon, Helen. "Childhood Sexual Abuse in Adult Female Psychotherapy Referrals." *British Journal of Psychiatry*, 1988; 152: 107-11.

Shengold, Leonard. *Soul Murder: The Effects of Childhood Abuse and Deprivation*. New Haven: Yale University Press, 1989.

Stendahl, Krister. "The Apostle Paul and the Introspective Conscience of the West." *Harvard Theological Review* 1963; 56: 199-215.

_____, ed. *Immortality and Resurrection*. New York: MacMillan & Co., 1958.

_____. "Immortality Is Too Much and Too Little." In Stendahl, *Meanings: The Bible as Document and Guide*. Minneapolis: Augsburg Fortress Press, 1984, pp. 193-202.

_____. *Paul Among Jews & Gentiles & Other Essays*. Minneapolis: Augsburg Fortress Press, 1976.

Strachey, James. "Appendix to Freud's Essay 'Resistances to Psycho-Analysis.'" In *The Standard Edition*, 19:223-24.

Terrell, Peter, Veronika Schnorr, Wendy V. A. Morris, and Roland Breisprecher. *Collins German-English, English-German Dictionary*. New York: Harper Collins, 1991.

Van der Kolk, Bessel. *Psychological Trauma*. Washington: American Psychiatric Press, 1987.

Vincent, M. O. "Christianity and Psychiatry: Rivals or Allies?" *Canadian Psychiatric Association Journal*, 1975; 20:527-32.

Weatherhead, Leslie D. *The Will of God*. Nashville: Abingdon Press, 1976.

Williams, David R., David B. Larson, Robert E. Buckler, Richard C. Heckmann, and C. M. Pyle. "Religion and Psychological Distress in a Community Sample." *Social Science and Medicine*, 1991; 32: 1257-62.

Winnicott, Donald W. *Home Is Where We Start From*. Edited by Clare Winnicott, Ray Shepherd, and Madeleine Davis. New York: W. W. Norton & Co., 1986.

_____. *Playing and Reality*. New York: Routledge, 1989.

_____. *Through Paediatrics to Psycho-Analysis*. New York: Basic Books, 1975.

Yalom, Irvin D. *Love's Executioner and Other Tales of Psychotherapy*. New York: Harper Collins, 1990.

Thou . . . hast sinned against thy **soul**.

(KJV: Habakkuk 2:10)

You have forfeited your **life**.

(NRSV: Habakkuk 2:10)

Order Form

Please send me:

☐ **Soul Psychology:** *How to Understand Your Soul in Light of the Mental Health Movement,* by Jeffrey H. Boyd, Cheshire, Conn.: Soul Research Institute, 1994. Price: $ 14.95

☐ **Affirming the Soul:** *Remarkable Conversations Between Mental Health Professionals and an Ordained Minister,* by Jeffrey H. Boyd (with Preface and Comments by Krister Stendahl), 1994. Price: $ 14.95

Last Name: ☐☐☐☐☐☐☐☐☐☐☐☐☐☐☐☐☐☐☐

First Name: ☐☐☐☐☐☐☐☐☐☐☐☐☐☐☐☐☐

Address: ☐☐☐☐☐☐☐☐☐☐☐☐☐☐☐☐☐☐☐

☐☐☐☐☐☐☐☐☐☐☐☐☐☐☐☐☐☐☐

City: ☐☐☐☐☐☐☐☐☐☐☐☐☐ State: ☐☐

Zip Code: ☐☐☐☐☐ — ☐☐☐☐

Daytime phone: ☐☐☐ — ☐☐☐ — ☐☐☐☐ _____
extension

Sales Tax: For book shipped to a Connecticut address, please add 6%.

Shipping & Handling: Book rate: $ 3.95 for the first book and $ 2.50 for each additional (may take 3-4 weeks). For bulk orders, air mail, or orders outside the USA, phone or write for shipping and handling costs. Prices subject to change as of 1996.

Total Amount Submitted: $ ☐☐☐.☐☐

Payment by   Check   Master Card   Visa

Card Number:

☐☐☐☐ ☐☐☐☐ ☐☐☐☐ ☐☐☐☐

Expiration Date: ☐☐ / ☐☐ Name on Card: ☐☐☐☐☐☐☐☐☐☐☐☐☐☐☐☐

Mail this form to:

Cardholder's Signature: _____

**Soul Research Institute
Department 2-A
P. O. Box 89
Cheshire, CT 06410
Phone/FAX (203) 250-9918**

Order Form

Please send me:

☐ *Soul Psychology: How to Understand Your Soul in Light of the Mental Health Movement*, by Jeffrey H. Boyd, Cheshire, Conn.: Soul Research Institute, 1994. Price: $ 14.95

☐ *Affirming the Soul: Remarkable Conversations Between Mental Health Professionals and an Ordained Minister*, by Jeffrey H. Boyd (with Preface and Comments by Krister Stendahl), 1994. Price: $ 14.95

Last Name: ☐☐☐☐☐☐☐☐☐☐☐☐☐☐☐☐

First Name: ☐☐☐☐☐☐☐☐☐☐☐☐☐☐☐

Address: ☐☐☐☐☐☐☐☐☐☐☐☐☐☐☐☐
☐☐☐☐☐☐☐☐☐☐☐☐☐☐☐☐

City: ☐☐☐☐☐☐☐☐☐☐☐☐☐☐ State: ☐☐

Zip Code: ☐☐☐☐☐ — ☐☐☐☐

Daytime phone: ☐☐☐ — ☐☐☐ — ☐☐☐☐   _____ extension

Sales Tax: For book shipped to a Connecticut address, please add 6%.

Shipping & Handling: Book rate: $ 3.95 for the first book and $ 2.50 for each additional (may take 3-4 weeks). For bulk orders, air mail, or orders outside the USA, phone or write for shipping and handling costs. Prices subject to change as of 1996.

Total Amount Submitted: $ ☐☐☐☐.☐☐

Payment by   Check   Master Card   Visa

Card Number: ☐☐☐☐ ☐☐☐☐ ☐☐☐☐ ☐☐☐☐

Expiration Date: ☐☐ / ☐☐   Name on Card: ☐☐☐☐☐☐☐☐☐☐☐☐☐☐☐

Cardholder's Signature:

_____

Mail this form to:

**Soul Research Institute
Department 2-A
P. O. Box 89
Cheshire, CT 06410
Phone/FAX (203) 250-9918**

Order Form

Please send me:

☐ **Soul Psychology:** *How to Understand Your Soul in Light of the Mental Health Movement,* **by Jeffrey H. Boyd, Cheshire, Conn.: Soul Research Institute, 1994.** Price: $ 14.95

☐ ***Affirming the Soul:*** *Remarkable Conversations Between Mental Health Professionals and an Ordained Minister,* **by Jeffrey H. Boyd (with Preface and Comments by Krister Stendahl), 1994.** Price: $ 14.95

Last Name: ☐☐☐☐☐☐☐☐☐☐☐☐☐☐☐

First Name: ☐☐☐☐☐☐☐☐☐☐☐☐☐☐☐

Address: ☐☐☐☐☐☐☐☐☐☐☐☐☐☐☐

☐☐☐☐☐☐☐☐☐☐☐☐☐☐☐

City: ☐☐☐☐☐☐☐☐☐☐☐☐ State: ☐☐

Zip Code: ☐☐☐☐☐ — ☐☐☐☐

Daytime phone: ☐☐☐ — ☐☐☐ — ☐☐☐☐ extension _____

Sales Tax: For book shipped to a Connecticut address, please add 6%.

Shipping & Handling: Book rate: $ 3.95 for the first book and $ 2.50 for each additional (may take 3-4 weeks). For bulk orders, air mail, or orders outside the USA, phone or write for shipping and handling costs. Prices subject to change as of 1996.

Total Amount Submitted: $ ☐☐☐ . ☐☐

Payment by   Check   Master Card   Visa

Card Number: ☐☐☐☐ ☐☐☐☐ ☐☐☐☐ ☐☐☐☐

Expiration Date: ☐☐ / ☐☐   Name on Card: ☐☐☐☐☐☐☐☐☐☐☐☐

Mail this form to:

Cardholder's Signature:

Soul Research Institute
Department 2-A
P. O. Box 89
_____ **Cheshire, CT 06410**
Phone/FAX (203) 250-9918

Order Form

Please send me:

☐ **Soul Psychology:** *How to Understand Your Soul in Light of the Mental Health Movement,* by Jeffrey H. Boyd, Cheshire, Conn.: Soul Research Institute, 1994.

Price: $ 14.95

☐ *Affirming the Soul: Remarkable Conversations Between Mental Health Professionals and an Ordained Minister,* by Jeffrey H. Boyd (with Preface and Comments by Krister Stendahl), 1994.

Price: $ 14.95

Last Name: ☐☐☐☐☐☐☐☐☐☐☐☐☐☐☐☐☐☐☐☐

First Name: ☐☐☐☐☐☐☐☐☐☐☐☐☐☐☐☐☐☐

Address: ☐☐☐☐☐☐☐☐☐☐☐☐☐☐☐☐☐☐☐☐

☐☐☐☐☐☐☐☐☐☐☐☐☐☐☐☐☐☐☐☐

City: ☐☐☐☐☐☐☐☐☐☐☐☐☐☐ State: ☐☐

Zip Code: ☐☐☐☐☐ — ☐☐☐☐

Daytime phone: ☐☐☐ — ☐☐☐ — ☐☐☐☐ extension _____

Sales Tax: For book shipped to a Connecticut address, please add 6%.

Shipping & Handling: Book rate: $ 3.95 for the first book and $ 2.50 for each additional (may take 3-4 weeks). For bulk orders, air mail, or orders outside the USA, phone or write for shipping and handling costs. Prices subject to change as of 1996.

Total Amount Submitted: $ ☐☐☐.☐☐

Payment by   Check   Master Card   Visa

Card Number: ☐☐☐☐ ☐☐☐☐ ☐☐☐☐ ☐☐☐☐

Expiration Date: ☐☐/☐☐   Name on Card: ☐☐☐☐☐☐☐☐☐☐☐☐☐☐

Mail this form to:

Cardholder's Signature: _____

Soul Research Institute
Department 2-A
P. O. Box 89
Cheshire, CT 06410
Phone/FAX (203) 250-9918